Medical Billing Networks and Processes

Medical Billing Networks and Processes

Profitable and Compliant Revenue Cycle Management in the Internet Age

Yuval Lirov

Affinity Billing Inc.
Marlboro, New Jersey

Affinity Billing Inc.
Marlboro, New Jersey

Library of Congress Cataloging-in-Publication Data
Lirov, Yuval
Medical Billing Networks and Processes: Profitable and Compliant Revenue Cycle Management in the Internet Age / Yuval Lirov
p. cm.
Includes bibliographical references and index
ISBN 978-0-9796101-3-4
1. Medical—Practice Management, Billing, etc.

Limit of Liability/Disclaimer of Warranty: This publication is designed to provide accurate and authoritative information in connection with the subject matter covered. While the publisher and author have used their best efforts in preparing this book, they make no representations or warranties with respect to the accuracy or completeness of the contents of this book and specifically disclaim any implied warranties of merchantability or fitness for a particular purpose. The contents of this publication involve the opinions and beliefs of the author, based on the author's experience in these matters, and should in no way be otherwise construed by the industries that are discussed herein or its participants. This publication is being sold with the understanding that the author is not engaged in rendering legal, accounting, coding, or other professional advice or service nor does he prescribe any treatment or strategy that should be tested without the advice of a professional. The author specifically disclaims any liability, damage, or risk of loss, personal or otherwise, which is incurred as a consequence, directly or indirectly, of the sale and distribution of this publication or use and application of any of the contents of this publication. If any expert assistance is required, the services of a competent professional person should be sought. Examples are generally descriptive and do not purport to be accurate in every regard. The practice management and healthcare industry is evolving rapidly, and all information should be considered time sensitive.

First Edition 2009
Printed in the United States of America

Interior Book Design and Copyediting by Alison F. Cohen
Illustrations by Natalia Pisano

To Shulamith, Victor, Mazal, Erez, Roy,
Reuven, Lori, Danielle, and Adam

Table of Contents

List of Figures

List of Tables

Foreword

I've been involved in medical billing as both a medical provider and a billing services provider for over 25 years. The one unchanging fact is that doctors don't get paid what they're owed.

Insurance companies and Medicare have not only cut compensation rates, they have systematically developed elaborate and arcane systems that make medical billing so complicated that individual physicians cannot hope to confront the forces arrayed against them.

Simple, off-the-shelf computer systems, or mom-and-pop billing services manned by minimally trained personnel, cannot successfully contend with the constantly changing and sophisticated systems designed to deny payments. Hundreds of insurance groups, with thousands of payment schedules, are beyond the expertise of even the most expensive solutions available. An alarming statistic is that 30% of medical bills are either denied or underpaid.[1]

I used to tell a joke that "there are no PhDs in medical billing." But Yuval Lirov represents a new paradigm for medical billing, which turns this joke on its head. He's a PhD in mathematics and computer science, with an unmatched expertise in modern transaction processing, who brought transformational technology to an industry mired in obsolete methods and thinking. Rather than surrender to the overpower-

[1] Walker, Larch, and Woodcock, *The Physician Billing Process*.

ing and relentless tactics of the insurance companies, he has designed a solution that matches the power, sophistication, and cost advantages of the insurance companies to finally give the advantage to the physician.

In *Medical Billing Networks and Processes*, Yuval identifies and analyzes the problems facing physicians, and then he offers his unique and proven solutions. *Medical Billing Networks and Processes* is the best book I've read for understanding and addressing the problems faced by physicians in their quest to be paid in a fair and timely manner.

This book is a service to all of those who wish to understand the billing process—and those who wish to address their own billing issues. This follow-up to his first book, *Practicing Profitability*, broadens the scope by bringing in more information relevant to a wider range of medical specialties as well as physical therapists. Insurance billing represents the vast majority of income for most physicians and therapists, yet they typically find themselves exerting less and less control over this vital portion of their income. Attempts by physicians and therapists to bill in their offices have become increasingly difficult and costly. Outsourcing billing, in many instances, gives up control as well as the ability to truly judge the quality of the billing services.

Yuval's solutions address these issues in a manner previously unavailable to the majority of practices. Continued changes make the issues in *Medical Billing Networks and Processes* timelier than ever.

—Douglas Cassel, MD
Vista Billing, LLC
Newport Beach, California

Acknowledgments

This book is a result of teamwork and hard work by several talented teams. Erez Lirov contributed countless ideas and led every aspect of system development and maintenance. Lori and Mazal Lirov worked right next to us, implementing it in practice. Roy Lirov contributed major portions of advertising and written and recorded training material. Doug Cassel, MD, introduced us to medical billing and, together with Bob Ettl, provided inspiration and support.

Hundreds of doctors, office managers, and lawyers generated a continuous flow of original requirements and comments. Special thanks to Scott Alenick, MD, of Pediatric Cardiology; Zelik Frischer, MD, clinical professor of urology at Stony Brook University School of Medicine; Ted Gutowski, MD, of Robert Wood Johnson University Hospital; Joseph Kamelgard, MD, of Lighter for Life; Vivian Kominos, MD, of Heart Specialists of Central Jersey; Glenn Laub, MD, chairman of cardiothoracic surgery at St. Francis Hospital in New Jersey; Michael Lewko, MD, chief medical officer at Care Management of St. Joseph Hospital; Gamil Makar, MD, director of Senior Health Partners; Michael McGinnis, MD, chairman of surgical pathology at Centrastate Medical Center; Prashant Pandya, MD, of Livingston Medical Associates; and Boris Petrikovsky, MD, chairman of the Department of Obstetrics & Gynecology at Nassau University Medical Center and professor of Obstetrics, Gynecology, and Reproductive

Medicine at Stony Brook University School of Medicine.

Finally, my sincere thanks and appreciation go to Natalia Pisano, the artist who illustrated the book, and Alison F. Cohen, my editor, who brought with her the highest book publishing standards and book preparation project management skills and who dramatically improved both my grammar and the overall clarity and flow of my writing.

About This Book

Your practice survives on its collections. Collections determine the value of your practice and define the difference between a thriving business and a "sleepy" or insolvent clinic.

According to the Office of Inspector General (OIG), an overall claims submission error rate in 2005 reached 67%, resulting in $285 million in improper payments.[2] Naturally, a similarly huge amount was also underpaid. *Medical Billing Networks and Processes* shows simple, pragmatic ways to reduce both underpayment and overpayment risks.

This book is aimed at healthcare providers who are tired of shrinking earnings and substandard billing performance and who are looking for systematic payment performance improvement. It creates awareness of the payer-provider conflict, lists specific strategies and techniques that payers use to keep providers' money, and then shows you how to leverage the "network effect" for improving those all-important collections numbers and building profitable practices.

Who needs this book? *You* do, if you are . . .

- **A practice owner** who is losing sleep because of shrinking collections, growing audit risk, and escalating overhead
- **An owner of a billing service company** who is unable to

[2] Office of Inspector General, *Health Care Fraud.*

profitably grow the business because of cutthroat offshore competition, talent scarcity, and escalating costs of personnel and technology

- **A practice manager** who is overwhelmed by thousands of billing service providers and armies of practice management consultants
- **A practice management consultant** who is intimidated by insurance companies and confused by hundreds of billing and electronic medical record (EMR) systems
- **A billing specialist** who is dreaming to start your own billing service and looking for a profitable business development and operating methodology
- **A medical coder** who is worried about the disappearing future of the coding specialty because of doctors using paper- or computer-based "superbills"
- **A healthcare practice compliance officer** who is afraid of impending audit, fraud potential, security and privacy violations, or data loss
- **A computer programmer** who is tired of being underpaid—and who wants to transition to a lucrative medical records or billing technology software firm
- **A student in a graduate healthcare management or administration program** who plans to become a practice management consultant
- **A physician or physical therapist** getting ready to start a practice

When we developed Vericle Billing System, we were concerned about the tremendous disparity rapidly building between the rising healthcare cost "tsunami" on one hand and dwindling doctors' compensation on the other hand. How can healthcare insurance premiums and payers' share value grow while providers earn less?

At the time, thousands of healthcare practices had separate billing systems. The result was thousands of small installations, all falling into the payer's methodology and leaving significant portions of the provider's money to the payer. We had to find a better way to collect payments than the stale, rote methods introduced by insurance companies, which aim toward paying less and keeping the physician's money for themselves. Because of our expertise in applying Straight-Through Processing (STP) methodology to telecommunications and financial management domains—which I documented in my earlier book, *Mission-Critical Systems Management* (Prentice Hall, 1997)—we focused on extending STP to healthcare. Our experiments extended far beyond developing new collections techniques. We gradually created Vericle, a comprehensive practice management system that integrates billing process management tools and a new, Internet-based billing and practice management philosophy.

Vericle's system uses centralized technology that serves hundreds of stand-alone billing services and healthcare clinics. With its emphasis on centralized tracking of payer performance from a single point of control, shared coding compliance rules, and accountable teamwork, Vericle's system demonstrates the "network effect" and performance improvements to billing companies and physician practices around the country.

What Will This Book Do for You?

This book will not teach you the basics of practice management, coding, billing, or compliance. For introductory material, there are excellent texts listed at the back of this book.[3] Medical practice is a busi-

---

3 See Aalseth, *Codebusters*; Buppert, *Primary Care Provider's Guide*; Burgos, *Medical Billing*; Delman, *Business of Chiropractic*; Reizer, *Up and Running*; Rowell and Green, *Understanding Health Insurance*; and Saner, *Understanding Compliance*.

ness, and doctors need to make strategic decisions about adding equipment, hiring other doctors, addressing specific kinds of patients, selection of referrals, marketing, etc. To learn how to use quantitative data to make such decisions, read *The Business of Medical Practice: Advanced Profit Maximization Techniques for Savvy Doctors* by David Edward Marcinko.

Medical Billing Networks and Processes takes over where these texts leave you; as you read this book, your view of billing will change. The Vericle system transforms the nature of the claims processing cycle. It provides an accountable approach to billing that places the practice owner firmly in control. The book documents our experience, and it provides structured direction on how to apply that experience in practice to improve your revenue and office management productivity.

I chose small-scale family practice examples because of relatively high processing volumes, low average claim payment value, and a uniquely high likelihood for audit. Together, these three aspects of medical practice combine for especially demanding conditions in terms of office automation.

This book evolves from *Practicing Profitability*, my earlier book on the same topic that primarily focused on managing chiropractic clinics. While skipping chiropractic-specific topics—e.g., care plans and point-of-service retail product sales—this book has more space to focus on traditional medical practice. I also include five invited chapters:

- A chapter on physician "Super Groups," legal entities that restore to physicians the rightful compensation and clinical autonomy to which they're entitled as plenary license holders. This is by Dennis J. Alessi, Esq., a partner in the West Orange, New Jersey, office of Mandelbaum, Salsburg, Gold, Lazris & Discenza, PC. Mr. Alessi chairs the Health Care Department of the firm and represents clients in all areas of healthcare law.

- A chapter on electronic medical records by Eric Fishman, MD, who is considered a world expert in the use of speech recognition in medical records production. His publication, *EHR Scope*, includes the largest compendium of EMR software.
- A chapter on integrating systems for practice management, electronic medical records, and billing by Joseph Kamelgard, MD. Dr. Kamelgard uniquely combines an education in medicine and engineering. He focuses on providing 21st-century tools to clinicians so they can deliver appropriate medical care to their patients while remaining profitable.
- Two chapters on ethical coding and billing practices, focusing on the liability risk management under the False Claims Act. These chapters were written by Erum Raza, Esq., an associate in the Princeton, New Jersey, office of Fox Rothschild LLP. Ms. Raza is a corporate attorney and CPA who specializes in healthcare law and business transactions.

Most chapters in this book outline specific implementation steps. The best way to benefit from the material is to follow these steps in your practice. Here's an example of how *Medical Billing Networks and Processes* teaches you to evaluate billing performance: Take a sheet of blank paper, and grab your last monthly billing report. On the paper, draw a graph with the y-axis (vertical) showing payments and the x-axis (horizontal) showing time as 30, 60, 90, and 120 days. Next, draw vertical bars on your graph, at 15-day increments, to show your actual payments (Figure 1).

A tight, narrow bell curve centered around 10–15 days means that your billing service has excellent performance. A wide, flat bell curve centered around 60–75 days means that payers take advantage of your practice—and you're leaving a significant portion of your reimbursement to the payers.

Figure 1. Payment Distribution Chart

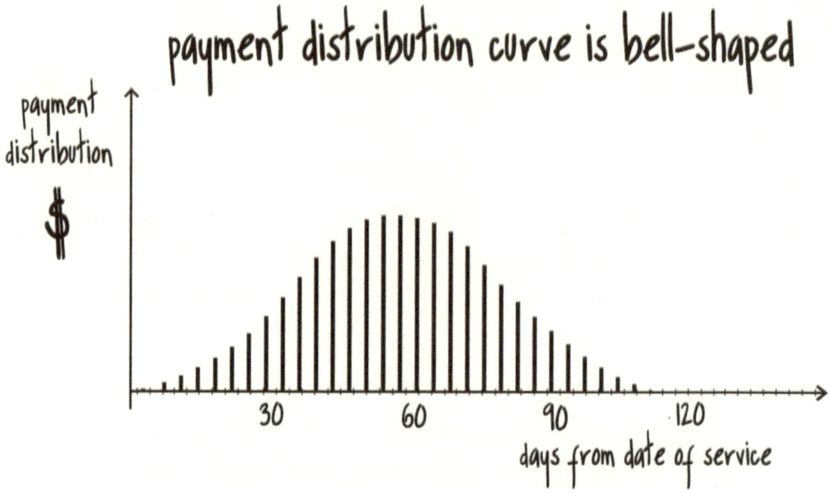

Payment distribution provides a visual indication of billing quality.

I welcome your feedback to help me improve future editions of this book. Please email your comments and suggestions via the Contact page at www.vericle.net.

Medical Billing Networks and Processes

Part I

Payer-Provider Adversity

Now, here, you see, it takes all the running you can do, to keep in the same place. If you want to get somewhere else, you must run at least twice as fast as that!

—The Queen
Through the Looking Glass
Lewis Carroll

You didn't go into healthcare to be "average." Like most good doctors, you're an optimist. You believe you can be a top producer and earn the highest possible compensation for your services. After all, you have excellent training and you're not afraid of hard work.

Yet your practice isn't making what you think it should be. What's gone wrong? And, more importantly, what, if anything, can you do about it?

Part I examines **why billing services fail to collect as promised**. It looks at what keeps so many otherwise talented, capable practice owners and managers from generating top revenue.

The good news is that billing performance can be improved—dramatically and permanently. But first you need to know where to begin and what needs fixing.

Ideally, the billing encounter should be viewed as a win-win situation. But a practice owner or billing manager who has spent time "in the trenches" knows that this is simply not the case. Insurance companies have adopted an adversarial approach to providers. Under the payer's "system," the goal is to keep as much as possible of the provider's money without violating the timely payment laws. Payers can delay claims processing, underpay, return for payment refunds, and impose penalties.

Modern medical billing started in 1984, when the Health Care Financing Administration (HCFA), now called the Centers for Medicare and Medicaid Services (CMS), first required providers to use the standard HCFA-1500 form and standard CPT codes to submit Medicare claims.

At first, HCFA forms were coded manually and submitted by mail, while the two key participants—namely, HCFA and Medicare—established the following reporting standards:

- 1988 – Medicare added the requirement to report ICD-9 on HCFA-1500 forms.
- 1989 – Medicare required all physicians to submit claims on behalf of Medicare patients, regardless of the physician's participation in the Medicare program.
- 1996 – HCFA developed Correct Coding Initiative (CCI) to promote national coding standards in terms of matching rules between ICD-9 and CPT codes.

Technology became the decisive weapon in the payer-provider conflict. Billing technology developed initially along three directions: data entry, claims processing (adjudication), and participant connectivity. By 1996, payers had already heavily invested in building electronic claims processing technology. Payers also almost completely eliminated their data entry costs by enabling electronic claims submissions and shifting claim coding costs to providers. To connect payers with providers and consumers, Jim Clark conceived Healtheon (now Emdeon), the first claims clearinghouse. Since its creation in 1996, Healtheon has evolved into the largest electronic claims clearinghouse, connected to thousands of payers.

Given the high cost of software in the late 1990s, provider-side claims processing software could not keep up with payers' technology, and it remained limited to electronic claims submission. Thousands of providers resorted to feature-poor, client-server installations. These are costly to install and maintain, and they're unable to match the payer's processing power. Yet other industries, such as telecommunications and investment banking, developed processes for millions of transactions across multiple remote participants. Straight-Through Processing (STP) emerged as the leading methodology to keep up with regulatory demands and massive transaction volumes.

Vericle was born in 2001. It was envisioned as an enabling technology for providers to match the awesome processing power available to the largest payers. Its centrally managed platform integrates medical office billing and front office functionalities with Internet connectivity, leveraging STP methodology.

Vericle tracks payer performance from a single point of control and shares compliance rules globally. Vericle also takes advantage of Software as a Service (SaaS) delivery models, improving operations control, turning a capital expense into an operating expense, and therefore improving a practice's balance sheet.

A centrally managed STP platform delivered under the SaaS model was bound to culminate in a qualitative service change. Thus in 2004, Vericle began consolidating operations for hundreds of stand-alone billing services and practices, igniting the network effect: Vericle users began gaining more value in step with its growing network.

Accordingly, Part I starts with a review of the key healthcare cost drivers and evidence of how provider compensation has failed to keep up with healthcare costs. Chapter 2 presents background information about several successful offline audits of payers that discovered systematic efforts to reduce provider compensation. Chapter 3 introduces the concept of the "payer-provider conflict" and outlines the need for a billing system that can level the playing field with the payers. Chapter 4 describes specific strategies and tactics used by payers to increase their profits and reduce costs, often at the expense of providers. Chapter 5 describes traditional billing systems in more detail, and it analyzes why they fail to match the payers' systems. Chapter 6 introduces billing networks—including Vericle—that aim to implement, in real time, payer audits similar to those described in Chapter 2; they do so by aggregating individual practice claim volumes and analyzing them using a centralized infrastructure. Chapter 7 describes Metcalfe's law, the "billing network effect," and the resulting economies of scale and specific benefits to individual practice owners/members of the billing network. The invited chapter by Dennis J. Alessi, Esq., a partner and chair of the Health Care Department at Mandelbaum, Salsburg, Gold, Lazris & Discenza, PC, concludes Part I; it focuses on legal aspects of creating physician "Super Groups."

Chapter 1

Why Providers' Revenues Failed to Keep Up with Rising Healthcare Costs?

Healthcare spending continues to rise at the fastest rate in our history. In 2005, total national healthcare costs rose 6.9%—twice the rate of inflation—reaching $2 trillion, or $6,700 per person.[4] Currently, total healthcare spending represents 16% of the gross domestic product (GDP). In the next decade, U.S. healthcare spending is expected to increase at similar levels, reaching $4 trillion in 2015.[5]

Many experts maintain that our healthcare system is costly because it's riddled with inefficiencies, excessive administrative expenses, inflated prices, poor management, waste, inappropriate care, and fraud.[6] However, at least three remaining key factors—namely, aging population, expensive medical innovation, and defensive care—contribute substantially to the overall cost picture.

Let's look at these three factors:

---

[4] Catlin, Cowan, and Heffler, "National Health Spending in 2005."

[5] Borger et al., "Health Spending Projections."

[6] National Coalition on Health Care, *Health Insurance Costs*.

1. **Aging population**

   In the United States, the proportion of the population aged 65 and over is projected to increase from 12.4% in 2000 to 19.6% in 2030. The number of people aged 65 years and over is expected to increase from approximately 35 million in 2000 to an estimated 71 million in 2030, and the number of people aged 80 and over is expected to increase from 9.3 million in 2000 to 19.5 million in 2030.[7]

   According to a United Nations report, "the growing number of older adults increases demands on the public health system and on medical and social services. Chronic diseases, which affect older adults disproportionately, contribute to disability, diminish quality of life, and increased health- and long-term-care costs."[8] As many as 125 million Americans have one or more chronic conditions (e.g., congestive heart failure, diabetes). Chronic diseases account for 75% of all healthcare expenditures.[9]

2. **Expensive medical innovation**
   a. The American biotechnology industry has surpassed pharmaceutical companies for the third straight year as the primary source of new medicines, and biotech revenue jumped nearly 18% from 2004 to 2005, reaching $63.1 billion.[10]
   b. The United States is the world's largest and wealthiest pharmaceutical market, accounting for around 48% of the world total. Per capita expendi-

---

[7] Goulding, Rogers, and Smith, "Public Health and Aging."

[8] United Nations, *Report of the Second World Assembly*.

[9] Burrill, *Biotech 2007*.

[10] Ernst & Young, *Double-digit growth*.

Figure 2. Aging Population in U.S.

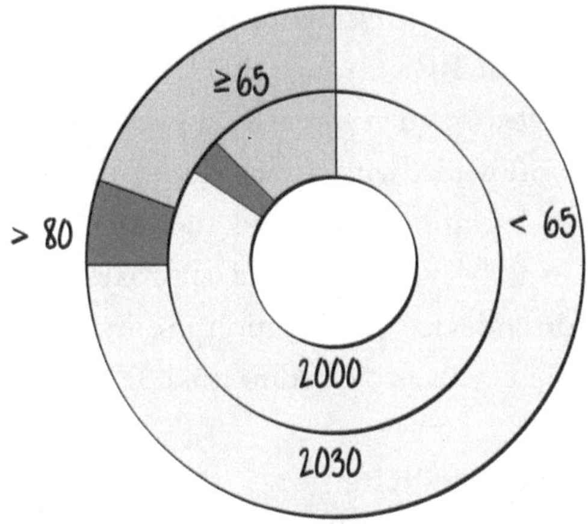

Population (in millions)

	2000	2030
≥65	35.0 (12.4%)	71.0 (19.6%)
> 80	9.3 (3.3%)	19.5 (5.4%)
< 65	238.0 (84.0%)	271.7 (75.0%)
total	282	362

By 2030, 19.6% of the U.S. population will be age 65 or over.[11]

ture on drugs was $1,069 in 2006, nearly double the level found in the rest of the world.[12]

c. An estimated 30% of new products under development are "combo products"—involving medical devices embedded with pharmaceutical or biologics components.[13] The combination products market

[11] Goulding, Rogers, and Smith, "Public Health and Aging."

[12] Espicom Business Intelligence, *Research and Markets.*

[13] Richter, *Combination Products.*

was estimated at $5.9 billion in 2004, and is expected to continue to grow at a compound annual rate of 10% through 2009. By that year, the market is expected to reach approximately $9.5 billion worldwide, with a majority of these revenues from drug-eluting stents and steroid-eluting electrodes.[14] In 2004, the U.S. held approximately 65% of the drug-device combination product market. By 2010, the U.S. is projected to hold 57% of that market.[15]

3. **"Defensive" medicine**

   President George W. Bush said the following in a 2004 speech: "One of the major cost drivers in the delivery of health care are these junk and frivolous lawsuits. The risk of frivolous litigation drives doctors—and hear me out on this—they drive doctors to prescribe drugs and procedures that may not be necessary, just to avoid lawsuits. That's called the defensive practice of medicine . . . See, lawsuits not only drive up premiums, which drives up the cost to the patient or the employer of the patient, but lawsuits cause docs to practice medicine in an expensive way in order to protect themselves in the courthouse. The defensive practice of medicine affects the federal budget. The direct cost of liability insurance and the indirect cost from unnecessary medical procedures raise the federal government's health care costs by at least $28 billion a year."[16]

Now let's observe the paradox. On one hand, the participants of every ancillary industry to healthcare—including insurance companies,

[14] Dubin, "A One-Two Punch."

[15] U.S. Food and Drug Administration, *FY 2007 Performance Report.*

[16] Bush, Speech at Baptist Health Medical Center.

high-tech and pharmaceutical engineers and scientists, and lawyers—have increased their profits in step with the rising costs of healthcare at an ever-accelerating pace.

On the other hand, medical practice owners—the actual healthcare providers—have not only failed to keep step with rising costs but lost a significant part of their income. In fact, between 1995 and 1999, at a time when most wages and salaries in the United States rose 3.5% after adjusting for inflation, average physician net income from the practice of medicine, adjusted for inflation, dropped 5%.[17] In 2006, the median compensation for specialty and primary physicians grew only 1.7% ($322,259) and 2% ($171,519), respectively; this was slower than the 3.2% increase in the Consumer Price Index (Figure 3).[18] In comparison, healthcare costs beat the inflation by 3.5% reaching the annual

Figure 3. The Growing Disparity between Physician Compensation and Healthcare Costs in 2006

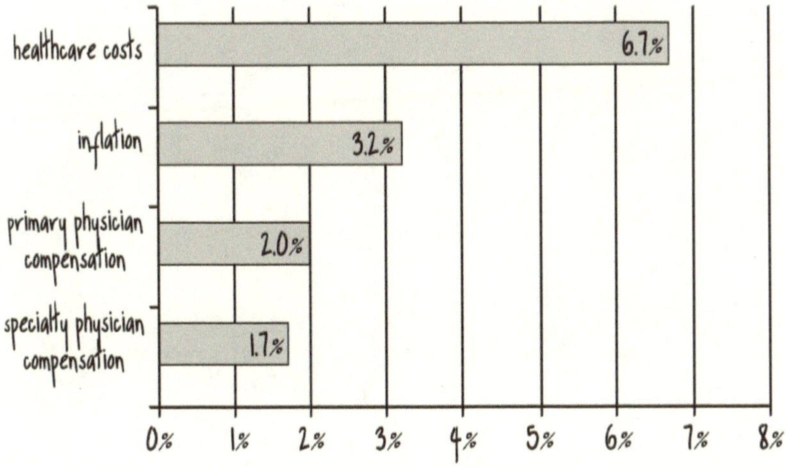

The annual increase in primary and specialty physician compensation during 2006 did not keep pace with healthcare costs and inflation.

---

[17] Reed and Ginsburg, *Behind the Times*.

[18] Medical Group Management Association, *Increases in Primary, Specialty Physician Compensation*.

growth rate of 6.7.[19]

While many experts are busy trying to find solutions to the problem of rising healthcare costs, we ask a different question: how can such a disparity be possible without a deliberate and systematic strategy against healthcare providers?

[19] Henry J. Kaiser Family Foundation, *Health Insurance Premium Growth*.

Chapter 2

Do Providers Need to Audit Payers?

A Sacramento-area surgeon couldn't schedule surgeries for more than six months because his contract wasn't loaded in the insurer's computer system. More than 200 of a family practice physician's patients received letters indicating incorrectly that he was no longer participating in the network; the physician lost about 25% of these patients and wasn't paid for about eight months. An insured patient spent 11 months trying to get claims paid for his family, including an autistic child; the insurer never specified what information was needed to make the denied claims eligible for payment.

Are these three isolated incidents, or are they symptoms of a growing problem with the entire providers' reimbursement system? The owners of healthcare practices easily recognize these painfully familiar symptoms. The better questions are: how are they related to the rising healthcare costs, and what can a provider do to help?

In 2005, national healthcare costs rose 6.9%—twice the rate of inflation—reaching $2 trillion. National healthcare costs are predicted to double to $4 trillion by 2015.[20] While key healthcare cost factors include an aging U.S. population, the arrival of new and expensive drugs and biotech devices, and defensive medicine, the insurance costs alone stand out as a key contributor. Exorbitant executive compensation has become a hallmark of the healthcare insurance industry; William McGuire, CEO of UnitedHealth Group, has reportedly received over $500 million since 1992, more than $1 billion in options, a lump-sum payout of $6.4 million upon leaving the company, and an annual pension of $5.1 million.[21] But such compensation can be easily justified on Wall Street when comparing it with outstanding insurance industry profits, in some cases reaching as high as 38% growth in earnings in the third quarter of 2006.[22]

The problem for any successful insurance company is how to make such growth sustainable? This question is difficult because the premium growth (68.4%) has disproportionally outpaced both inflation (16.4%) and workers' earnings (18.2%) during the same period (2001–2006), making it impossible to continue to raise premiums without losing major segments of the insured population.[23] Between 2000 and 2007, the average annual employer-sponsored group premium rose 81% for individual coverage (from $2,471 to $4,479) and 88% for family coverage (from $6,438 to $12,106).[24]

Without the ability to attract new clients or further raise insurance premiums, cost reduction becomes the next most important approach for insurance companies to enhance profitability. Such cost reduction can be done in a variety of ways, which I'll conveniently divide into strategic and tactical or opportunistic approaches.

---

[20] National Coalition on Health Care, *Facts on Health Care Costs.*

[21] Phelps and Serres, "McGuire's Deal."

[22] UnitedHealth Group, "UnitedHealth Group Reports Record Third Quarter."

[23] Henry J. Kaiser Family Foundation, *The Uninsured.*

[24] Ibid.

Strategic Insurer's Arsenal

The creation of an oligopsony through consolidation is the main weapon in the strategic arsenal of insurance companies. An oligopsony exists when providers (in this case, physicians) significantly outnumber buyers (insurance companies), enabling the insurance companies to dictate prices because of reduced competition. Take, for example, PacifiCare's $9.2 billion merger with UnitedHealth Group in late 2005, which created a vast network of HMO and PPO plans covering more than three million Californians. Today, three plans alone (United-Healthcare, WellPoint, and Aetna) cover 77.7 million insured lives. This oligopsony allows the systematic and continuous cost reduction without extra investment. Some examples of this are the annual cut of allowed rates (the average reimbursement for E&M allowable dropped 10% in 2006 and another 6.5% in 2007[25]), payment suspension for specific procedures (such as EKG tests for routine physicals), offering "all or none" participation alternatives, or the creation of "tiered networks" that profile providers and incentivize patients to see lower-cost providers.

Tactical Insurer's Weapons

Increasing billing process complexity, inventing new reasons for denial through arcane terminology, disparate data formats, and modifications of CPT/ICD codes and medical necessity rules—these are all examples of tactical methods designed to increase providers' costs for both billing and follow-up and to reduce the payments at the expense of practice owners. These methods need continuous investment in personnel training, better process management, and improved technology to keep them effective as providers begin building more sophis-

---

[25] Moore, "The 2006 Fee Schedule Survey."

ticated systems to scrub and analyze claims and to discover payment discrepancies and irregularities.

Provider Response

Returning to the three incidents mentioned earlier, California's joint Department of Managed Health Care and Insurance Department determined that these are not isolated cases. They analyzed 1.1 million paid claims from June 2005 to May 2007 that covered about 190,000 members of PacifiCare's HMO and PPO plans, and they discovered that 30% of the HMO claims were wrongly denied and 29% of the disputes with doctors were handled incorrectly. PacifiCare paid out over $1 million and was fined additional $3.5 million.[26]

A year earlier, in 2007, the New Jersey Department of Banking and Insurance (NJDOBI) fined Aetna almost $9.5 million for paying certain out-of-network providers—limited to hospital, emergency, and approved out-of-network consultants—at 125% of Medicare rather than the providers' billed charges. NJDOBI also ordered Aetna to directly pay the affected providers' billed charges, in reparation, for certain services rendered out of network.[27]

In a separate incident, New York Attorney General Andrew M. Cuomo said that "he was investigating whether the nation's health insurance companies had systematically forced patients to pay more than they should when using doctors or hospitals outside of their insurer's networks."[28] Cuomo stated that he believed "there was an industry-wide scheme perpetuated by some of the nation's largest health insurers to deceive and defraud consumers" and that the scheme had lasted over "a decade, potentially adding hundreds of millions of dollars to

---

[26] Chan, "PacifiCare Fined."

[27] Skelton, *Aetna Ordered by NJDOBI*; New Jersey Department of Banking and Insurance, "Aetna Target."

[28] Abelson, "New York Investigates."

the out-of-pocket medical expenses of the nation's consumers."[29]

Nancy H. Nielsen, MD, president-elect of the American Medical Association, commended the investigation and said that the practice "is primarily unfair to consumers."[30] Linda Lacewell, head of Cuomo's Healthcare Industry Taskforce, said, "To date, we have found that health insurers consistently underpay consumers for their out-of-network medical expenses, and they do it through deception, manipulation of data and outright fraud."[31]

The issue at stake is how health insurers determine a usual, customary, and reasonable (UCR) payment for an out-of-network doctor's services. According to Cuomo, a six-month investigation found that Ingenix operated a defective and manipulated database that most major health insurers used to set reimbursement rates for out-of-network medical expenses. The probe also found that two UnitedHealth units dramatically underreimbursed members for out-of-network medical expenses by using Ingenix data.[32]

In a typical system, when a patient member goes out of network, insurers pay 80% of reasonable and customary charges, and the patient pays the remaining 20%. But in the Ingenix case, if the UCR was lower than what the doctor charged, then the patient ended up paying 20% of the reasonable and customary sum, *plus* the balance billed by the doctor.

For example, if the fair market rate in the New York metropolitan area was $200 for a 15-minute doctor visit for a common illness, but the Ingenix rate was only $77, then UnitedHealth's 80% payment would be only $62 (80% of $77). The consumer would end up paying $138 ($200 minus $62), instead of $40 (20% of $200).

---

[29] Ibid.

[30] NewsInferno.com, *Health Insurance Companies.*

[31] Office of the Attorney General, State of New York, *Cuomo Announces Industry-wide Investigation.*

[32] Ibid.

Lacewell said the Ingenix data was "rigged" in various ways. For example, Ingenix didn't audit the data it received from other insurers, who deleted some higher doctor charges before submitting the data. According to Lacewell, Ingenix itself deleted more high charges—valid ones—than low charges.

"This is a picture of conflict of interest from top to bottom," Lacewell said at a press conference, with a chart showing the interrelationship of Ingenix, UnitedHealth, and other insurers. "Every single player on this chart has an interest in keeping rates low. Nobody on this chart has an interest in keeping rates at a fair rate for consumers."[33]

In summary, providers need new and effective approaches to mobilize both legal and organizational talent to reverse their revenue decline. Legal methods battle market conditions like oligopsony, while large-scale medical billing networks aggregate claim volumes and create resulting economies of scale to enable analytical discovery of underpayments.

[33] Office of the Attorney General, State of New York, *Cuomo Announces Industry-wide Investigation*.

Chapter 3

Whose System Are You Following?

When two people tango, only one leads.
—Sign at dance studio

In the "provider-payer tango"—Vericle's metaphor for a claim-payment interaction—there are always two systems at work: the provider's system and the payer's system. To lead in this process, you must have, and use, a billing system that works. Merely submitting claims and then placing yourself in the arms of the payer, waiting to get paid, is not enough.

Healthcare insurance businesses continued to boom in 2006, mostly at the expense of both providers and patients. Two key aspects dominate the business background for insurers in 2006:

1. **Insurers must meet tougher profit margin benchmarks.** For instance, UnitedHealthcare saw its earnings rise 38% in the third quarter of 2006 alone.[34] To keep its

---

[34] Moore, "2006 Fee Schedule Survey."

share value growing, UnitedHealthcare had to demonstrate still better performance in the third quarter of 2007.

2. **Insurers approach the limit of their ability to grow premiums.** In 2001–2006, premiums increased disproportionately compared with inflation and workers' earnings growth. For instance, health insurance premiums increased 65.8% between 2001 and 2006, while inflation grew 16.4% and workers' earnings increased 18.2% during the same period (Figure 4).

Figure 4. Disproportionate Growth of Insurance Premiums

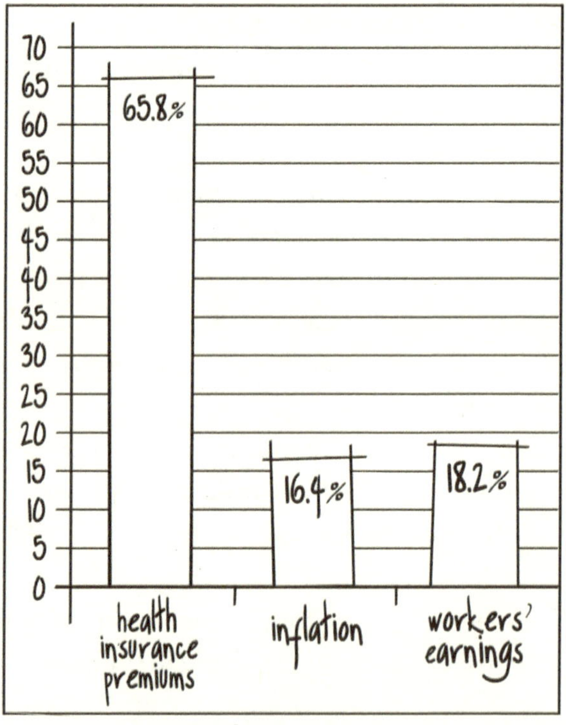

Health insurance premiums grew faster than inflation and workers' earnings from 2001 to 2006.

The motive in business is always profit, but insurance companies have it particularly rough. They play in a massively regulated, traditionally altruistic industry where they are the only for-profit game in town. Against all odds, they aggressively pushed their way to the top. But now, as Wall Street sweethearts, they have stepped through the looking glass into a world that seems to keep pace, no matter how fast they run. The faster they grow profits, the higher they drive expectations, leaving them increasingly desperate for new ideas to generate revenue.

Practice owners and billing service managers must assume responsibility for the current sad state of provider-payer relations. The efficacy of your system determines whether you lead or follow in the provider-payer tango. To take control, you must know what's happening at each step. You also must be comfortable in a leadership role. Vericle's research shows that most practice owners and managers struggle, and often fail, because they don't know how to be in control of the payment process.

Payers develop their current system in response to their business needs. Fair or unfair, the onus is on the provider and/or billing service, not the insurer. Rather than complain, you have to learn to thrive within the insurer's constraints. If the insurer's system can derail your billing efforts, then you need to adopt a modern, more effective billing system. It's that simple.

This book shows a better way. You may not get every claim paid—however, by using our system, you'll get *more* claims paid, and you'll certainly know what's happening to each one at every step. But first, you must understand how and why the payer's system works so well.

Chapter 4

The Payer's System

Payers have developed a simple but effective system to seize control of, and rapidly derail, a significant portion of billing efforts (Figure 5).

Figure 5. Uneven Playing Field between Payers and Providers

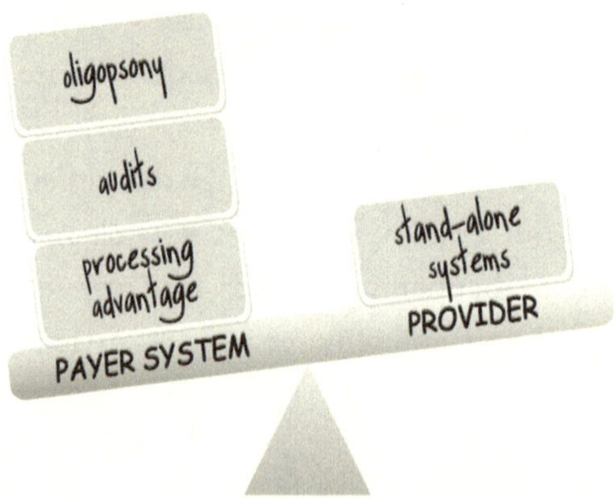

Resource and processing volume disparities lend a strategic advantage to payers.

Large-scale financial and technology infrastructure resources available to payers enable them to consolidate. These lend them a unique price control advantage, known as oligopsony, along with multiple added sources of revenue, such as underpayments, refunds, and penalties.

Payers typically employ the following strategies:

1. Increase billing service costs with added complexity and new reasons for denial.
2. Reduce allowed fees.
3. Increase leverage over providers through consolidation.
4. Underpay claims.
5. Return for post-payment audits, demand refunds, and impose penalties.

Strategy 1: Increase Billing Service Costs with Added Complexity and New Reasons for Denial

Payers use obscure and confusing terminology and disparate data formats. Deciphering payer messages requires sophisticated technology, skilled personnel, and time.

Payers also report only one error at a time. So, once you correct that error and resubmit the claim, payers get another chance for a new delay, based on a "newly discovered" error.

Next, payers frequently modify both formats and regulatory compliance rules (Correct Coding Initiative, or CCI, and local medical review policy, or LMRP). Discovering changes and implementing them in your system requires both investment and time. For instance, in January 2007, thousands of physicians discovered they were having trouble getting Medicare to pay for services billed under the codes 99303 and 99333. What were they doing wrong? The answer: Medicare deleted codes 99301–99303 from CPT in 2007, forcing the physicians to review the new 99304–99306 codes in an up-to-date CPT code book. The 99331–99333 codes were also deleted in 2007, so physicians needed to review the new 99324–99328 codes.

This is just one example of a systematic strategy to reduce or delay physician payments by complicating, changing, or otherwise raising physicians' costs of claims payment processes. This way, payers confront providers with a lose-lose dilemma of expensive process maintenance on the one hand and forfeited payments on the other. A practice that ignores the changes will face increased claims underpayments and rejection rates as well as higher audit risk exposure. But staying current with format and coding rules requires continuous and expensive billing system upgrades and frequent re-education of billing personnel.

Payer's profits can also be directly proportional to payment delays: the longer the delay, the higher the profit. A quick review of basic insurance financial performance metrics helps us understand the delay dynamic. An insurance company offers clients a premium based on the expected cost of caring for them, plus a markup for administrative costs and profit. Accordingly, most analysts use three metrics to measure financial performance of an insurance company:

1. **Administrative cost ratio (ACR)** – The ratio of administrative and sales expenses to the total income from premiums.
2. **Medical loss ratio (MLR)** – The ratio of medical expenses to income from premiums.
3. **Investment ratio (IR)** – Net investment income divided by revenue from premiums and fees.

For example, Aetna showed the following performance in 2007:

Premiums and fees	$25.5 billion
MLR	72%

ACR	21%
Combined ratio	93%
Implied operating margin	7%[35]

Note that other factors, especially legal fees, also influence profitability. But an insurer can actually turn a profit even if the cost of administration and insurance claims exceeds the premiums it collects. It does so by investing income *on the float* in stocks and bonds; the "float" is the time between when a client pays a premium and when the client needs payment for medical expenses. When we add MLR and ACR in the above example, we see that without any investment, Aetna would earn a 7% profit on its premiums alone. Nonetheless, Aetna takes advantage of the float and earns about 7% net interest income on the premiums—bringing its total profit margin to around 14% (ignoring taxes and other revenue sources):

Premium	7%
Interest on premium	7%
Total	14%

In this example, half of Aetna's profit margin in 2006 originated on the float.[36]

Insurance companies have often accused doctors of submitting incomplete and inaccurate claims, and they've justified the delays with the time needed to discover fraudulent claims. But some states have found insurance companies guilty of, and have penalized them for, intentionally delaying payments to profit from the float. For instance, as early as 1999, UnitedHealthcare paid Georgia $123,000, and Coventry Health Care of Georgia (formerly Principal Health Care of Georgia)

[35] Wikinvest, *Aetna*.

[36] Ibid.

and Prudential HealthCare Plan of Georgia paid nearly double that amount.[37]

The payer-related component of the medical billing process costs an average of 8% to 10% of a provider's collections.[38] This component includes claim generation, scrubbing, electronic submission to payers, payment posting, denial identification, follow-up, and appeal. By complicating the process, payers increase the likelihood of failing the payment and winning the subsequent appeal process. Providers face the lose-lose choice of either expensive medical billing process upgrades or forfeiture of denied payments.

Strategy 2: Reduce Allowed Fees

Average physician reimbursement from billing Medicare and commercial payers dropped 17% from 2002 to 2006. From 2005 to 2006, allowed amounts (Figure 6) for E&M visits alone dropped 10% nationally, 27% in the Northeast, and 20% in the Northwest.[39]

Strategy 3: Increase Leverage over Provider through Consolidation

It's harder to drop a contract with low allowed amounts when there are fewer remaining payers. Consolidation in the insurance industry reduces competition among payers for physicians' services (hence, oligopsony), allowing payers to pay less to providers. Today, 73% of the insured population are covered by just three plans; the top 10 health plans cover 106 million lives, while three plans—United, WellPoint, and Aetna—together cover 77.7 million lives. In 2006, the consolidation rate accelerated. For instance, UnitedHealthcare Group pur-

---

[37] Guglielmo, "Prompt-Pay Laws."

[38] McKay and Lemak, "Analyzing Administrative Costs."

[39] Moore, "2006 Fee Schedule Survey."

Figure 6. Billed, Allowed, Adjusted, and Paid Amounts

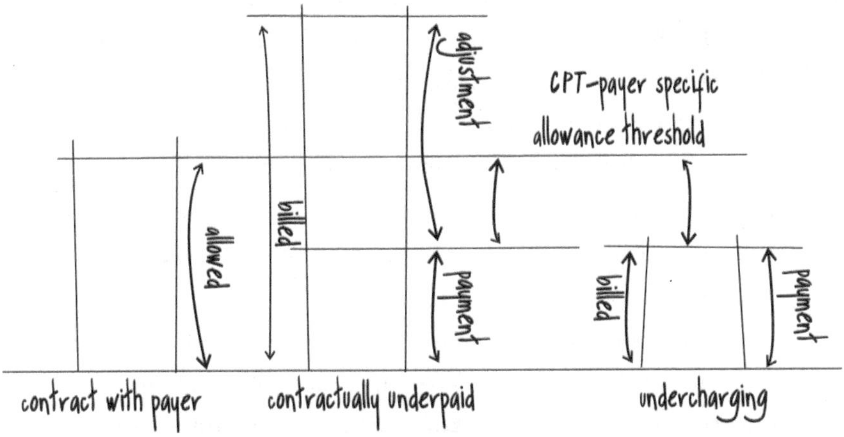

While excessive adjustment and overly conservative coding cause underpayment, providers are paid less simply by reducing allowed amounts.

chased 11 plans, including MetLife, PacifiCare, and Oxford.[40] Turning down a contract offered by a payer that controls such a large portion of the population results in giving up significant revenue from medical billing.

To drive providers into networks with lower allowed amounts, payers invented the "enrollee payment program." For instance, UnitedHealthcare announced a new national policy to discontinue direct payment of medical billing to out-of-network providers. Effective July 1, 2007, under the Pay the Enrollee program, UnitedHealthcare directs out-of-network benefit checks to the insured member rather than nonparticipating providers. As hard as it is to collect from the insurer, surely having to chase the actual patient for payment is harder and more costly, and it results in even lower collections.

This policy forces the providers to choose between chasing the patients for payments or joining the payer's network. In both cases, the

---

[40] Ibid.

provider loses some earned revenue. Oxford Health Plans, a UnitedHealthcare company, implemented the Pay the Enrollee policy on April 1, 2006. According to the Oxford website announcement, Oxford may refuse to honor the assignment of benefits for claims from nonparticipating providers pursuant to language in the Certificate of Coverage. If enrollees choose to receive out-of-network treatment, the claim reimbursement may be sent directly to the enrollee. In such cases, the nonparticipating provider is instructed to bill the covered enrollee for services rendered.[41]

Additionally, if patients continue to use out-of-network labs, physicians could face sanctions, including a "change of eligibility" in UnitedHealthcare's pay-for-performance and quality-rating programs, a "decreased fee schedule," or termination from the plan's network.

Once the provider is in the network, the payers implement profiling techniques to identify inefficient physicians. A recent Government Accountability Office (GAO) study examined 10 healthcare purchasers with profiling systems to determine whether inefficient physicians could be identified. After identifying inefficient physicians, the payers provided incentives to improve efficiency, such as the following:

- Educating physicians to encourage more efficient care
- Designating in physician directories those physicians who have met efficiency and quality standards
- Dividing physicians into tiers based on efficiency, and giving enrollees financial incentives to see physicians in their particular tiers
- Providing physicians bonuses, or imposing penalties, based on efficiency and quality standards
- Excluding inefficient physicians from the network

---

[41] Pérez-Peña, "When Choice of a Doctor."

Providers face the lose-lose choice of seeing fewer patients or accepting lower rates.

Strategy 4: Underpay Claims

Partial denials cause the average medical practice to lose as much as 11% of its revenue.[42] Denial management is difficult because of the complexity of denial causes, payer variety, and claim volume. Denial risk varies with different classes of claims, depending on claim complexity, temporary constraints, and payer idiosyncrasies.

For complex claims, most payers pay the full amount for one item, but only part of the remaining items, which creates opportunities for underpayment. Temporary constraints often cause payment errors because constraints are misapplied. Payer idiosyncrasies may arise when payers have different interpretations of CCI bundling rules or the coverage of certain services. (Learn more about this in Chapter 19.)

Strategy 5: Return for Post-Payment Audits, Demand Refunds, and Impose Penalties

The top two revenue-boosting wells for payers are drying up. Premium wars preclude insurers from raising rates, and recently enacted timely payment laws limit how long they can withhold repayment to earn interest as they had in the past. To meet profit expectations and still play within the new rules, insurers have decided to pursue the reimbursements *after* they are paid.

The Justice Department recovered a record $3.1 billion in fraud and false claims in 2006.[43] If payer audits seem like old news to you, take another look at the numbers in Table 1. It's an undeniably un-

---

42 Wang, "A Cost-benefit Analysis"; Waymack, "Harnessing the Power of e-Commerce."

43 U.S. Department of Justice. *Justice Department Recovers.*

scrupulous game. And if you're a billing service provider, you should know about it—because unless you're actively working to manage audit exposure, your clients are at risk.

Table 1. Fraud Statistics			
Year	New Matters	Judgments	Average Judgment
1993	61	$155,323,165	$2,546,281
1997	347	$920,350,127	$2,652,306
2000	260	$912,388,758	$3,509,188
2003	243	$1,825,406,640	$7,511,962

Source: U.S. Department of Justice (2006). *Justice Department Recovers Record $3.1 Billion in Fraud and False Claims in Fiscal Year 2006.*

If your skepticism has led you to the "rational" rebuttal that audits are expensive for everyone, rest assured that the invisible hand (gloved in technology) has helped insurers overcome this traditional obstacle. Driven by the simple goal of reducing the cost of identifying audit targets, insurers began building claims databases. With the advent of electronic submission, this became almost costless. As with many purportedly win-win propositions we've seen from insurers, electronic submission has proven to be a wolf in sheep's clothing. As providers submit claims to be paid, insurers simply add each claim to their growing database, and their computer science geeks regularly crank out reports that give executives a bird's-eye view of all their providers.

Invariably, providers are in denial about their exposure, and insurers are quick to comfort them. They'll tell you that audits are an unfortunate but necessary tactic for keeping fraud in check, implying that honest providers have nothing to worry about. But insurers are not crusaders for truth and justice. Providers need to understand that **the payer's motive is money, the payer's means is a gargantuan statistical database, and every provider is an opportunity**.

Healthcare finance insiders call this a Big Brother system, and, setting aside the melodramatic implications of such a name, it's easy to see why. Table 2 presents a short list of the types of reports generated by insurance companies.

Table 2. Audit Triggers – Profiling Methodology	
Stage	**Report**
Pre-Payment Review	CCI and LMRP rules Inter-claim, intra-claim, cross-claim Lifetime duplicates Date range duplicates Re-bundling Modifier codes E&M crosswalk Visit level
Post-Payment Audit	Procedure repetition High payments per day Surge analysis Unusual modifiers Unusual procedure rates Geographic improbabilities 5/50 patterns
External Resources	Provider watch lists OIG sanctions databases High-risk address databases

While executives have a soft spot for pretty charts, the true power of such a system is its ability to drill into the data and find outliers. (When they talk about this type of tool, information systems specialists use jargon like data mining and online analytical processing, or OLAP.) The system automatically pinpoints providers who are "easy audit targets" for one of the following reasons:

- They're doing something that's different from the pack.
- They lack the infrastructure for systematic denial follow-up.
- They lack compliant medical notes.

In summary, it's a fact of life: an ineffective billing system allows payers take the lead in the provider-payer tango and keep some of your practice revenue.

Chapter 5

Traditional Billing Systems

If you're like most practice owners or managers today, you use some form of the traditional billing systems that have been evolving since the birth of claim-based physician reimbursement. While these systems may use many different technologies, their underlying structures remain remarkably consistent: billing and coding personnel learn to code CMS-1500 forms, submit claims, review "scrubbing" and accounts receivable reports, call insurers to inquire about payment status, and call providers for missing data.

If you use a traditional billing approach and find yourself frequently falling victim to the payer's system instead of your own, you have plenty of company. Here are a few reasons why:

- Traditional billing systems **limit the provider's role** in the provider-payer tango, and they transfer the payment and decision initiative to the payer. Except for the initial claim submission, providers are completely passive at every step (Figure 7). You wait for the payer to review the claim, wait to receive the errors, wait for the review of the corrected submission, and wait, and wait. By waiting for the payer to determine if, when, and how much of the claim will be paid, you waste valuable time and further reduce the chances of getting the claim paid.

- In our experience, the average claim error rate without professional assistance is about 45%–55%. If your only method of finding errors is to submit the claim to the payer and wait for the payer's response, you'll need multiple submission cycles for each claim until you eradicate every error.
- By delaying your own response to a billing operator's query for claim clarification, you again waste valuable time and further reduce the chances of getting the claim paid.

Figure 7. Traditional Billing Model

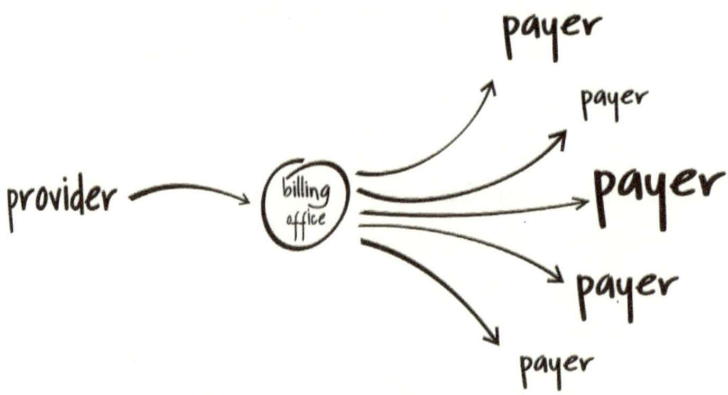

The traditional billing model confines providers to a passive role in the payer-provider tango, limited to claim submission and waiting for information from the payer.

- If your billing operator delays follow-up or selectively follows up on big-balance claims only, you may be doing the following:
    - **Encouraging** the payer to keep accumulating a

significant portion of your revenue

- **Increasing your audit risk** as you signal the payer that you might not have an adequate infrastructure to properly document every patient visit, just as you're unable to discover underpayments

- If you don't manage the individual productivity of billing personnel, you create three kinds of opportunities for the payers to keep your money:
  - You deprive your billing personnel of improving their skills and productivity. You simply don't know what the person working for you has done to get the claim paid and how long each action took.
  - Without "grand error" perspective, you prevent your entire billing infrastructure from improving its performance, and you're unable to keep up with the payers that frequently change formats and billing compliance requirements.
  - You encourage the billing office to simply collect fees only on uncontested and easily paid claims, forfeiting payments of problematic claims without even making any effort to collect.

A recent American Medical Association (AMA) study found that doctors spend 14% of the fees they receive from insurance companies and Medicare on the process of collecting those fees, adding more than $200 billion (about 10%) a year to the nation's healthcare costs.[44] Sadly, about 30% of over five billion claims generated annually are rejected—and surprisingly, only 50% of the rejected claims are ever re-

[44] Girion, "AMA Calls Physician Reimbursements Flawed."

submitted.[45] Note that physicians are giving up this revenue in addition to losing revenue because of the annual cuts of allowed fees. (Since 2000, health insurance premiums increased by 73% compared with cumulative increases in inflation and wages of about 15%. Yet physician's inflation-adjusted incomes dropped by 7% from 1995 to 2003.[46])

Why are the costs of collecting the earned fees so high—and why, adding insult to injury, do providers often skip resubmitting rejected claims?

Insurance companies would like us to think that billing costs are high because of inefficiencies, and they're quick to blame the doctors. According to UnitedHealthcare spokesman Gregory Thompson, "data show there is often a significant lag time between when services are provided and physician claims are submitted."[47] Another often-cited reason for delays and underpayments is the time that doctors take to resubmit claims or provide additional information upon the insurer's request.

But a recent AMA "report card" shows a wide variance between various payers in terms of payment accuracy and timeliness, ranging from 61% to 87% of the time.[48] Such a wide variance contradicts the "physician's inefficiency" theory. If this theory were true, then the more-efficient physicians would lose less money on rejections than others, and this would be uniform across all payers. Conversely, since the largest insurance companies are present in most states and are exposed to the vast majority of physicians and their claim delays, the differences in underpayments and denials must be attributed, first of all, to the differences in payers' business strategies and processes—and not to inefficiencies in the provider's office.

For instance, a simple calculation shows that systematic claim de-

---

[45] Walker, Larch, and Woodcock, *Physician Billing Process.*

[46] Herzlinger, *Who Killed Health Care?*

[47] Girion, "AMA Calls Physician Reimbursements Flawed."

[48] Von Bergen, "AMA Issues Report Card."

nial is beneficial to payers when the cost of rework outweighs the benefit of resubmitting the claim.[49] Let's assume the following:

$130	Initial charge
$55	Allowed amount
$29	Service cost
$6	Initial claim preparation and mail cost
$25	Claim rework cost

If the claim is paid in full after the contractual adjustment from $130 to $55, the profit would be as follows:

$55	Allowed amount
$35	Total initial practice costs ($29 plus $6)
$20	Practice income

But if the payer denies part of the claim—say, $30—then the provider has to choose between the options in Table 3.

Table 3. Provider Alternatives for Partial Claim Denial

	Do Nothing	Rework/ Repeat Denial	Rework/ Additional Payment
Total initial practice costs	($35)	($35)	($35)
Initial reimbursement	$25	$25	$25
Claim rework cost	$0	($25)	($25)
Additional reimbursement	$0	$0	$30
Practice income (loss)	($10)	($35)	($5)

As Table 3 shows, the provider can do the following:

1. Leave it alone, and lose $10 on the entire incident.

---

[49] Walker, Larch, and Woodcock, *Physician Billing Process*.

2. Rework it, and then risk losing even more:
    a. Lose $35 if there's a repeat denial.
    b. Lose $5 if the payer chooses to pay the previously denied part of the claim.

In other words, depending on the claim rework costs, denial amount, and repeat denial odds or claim rework efficacy, it may be in the provider's best interest to minimize losses by abandoning the denied claim instead of working the denial. Therefore, rational payers will deny a higher number of claims; they count on the good business sense of rational providers who will rework only a small subset of the denied claims, specifically those claims that they can justify with a quick cost-benefit calculation, such as the aforementioned example. Rational payers' behavior like this explains the AMA findings much better than any inefficiency on the provider's side.

To justify rework of every denial and to eliminate a financial incentive for payers to deny claims, providers need systems with low claim rework costs and high rework efficacy. To "educate and empower physicians so they are no longer at the mercy of a chaotic payment system that takes countless hours away from patient care" requires a leveled playing field for both providers and payers.[50] And leveling the playing field with the payers requires equal footing in terms of strategies, processes, and resources. Otherwise, if you follow a traditional billing system, you'll fall into the payer's system and wind up doing what the payer expects—i.e., you will leave a significant part of your money with the payer.

---

[50] William Dolan, MD, AMA board member, in Japsen, "AMA to Rate Business Practices."

Chapter 6

The Vericle System – A Better Way

To get the vast majority of claims paid in full and on time, you must employ a billing system that matches the power of the payer's system! The Vericle Billing System (Figure 8) is a no-nonsense approach to billing that frames the provider-payer tango as a business interaction among equals. The practice owner and manager who uses the Vericle system gains situational control in a conflict-ridden business environment.

Figure 8. The Vericle System

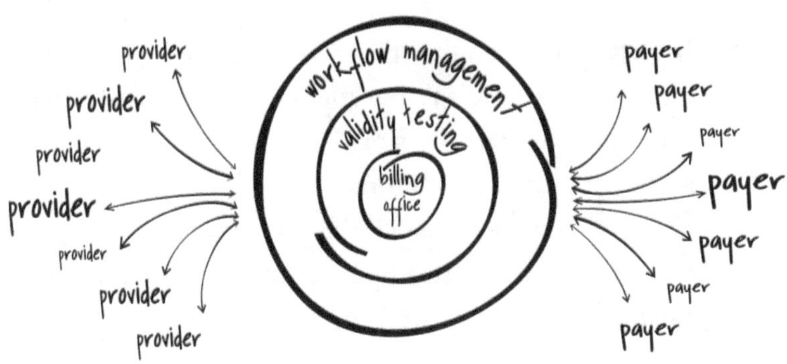

The Vericle system allows providers to maintain process control and create economies of scale.

Instead of catching up with payers' changes and depending on favors for mission-critical payment information, you gain an accountable mechanism for getting your claims paid. The effect is based on two principles: (a) meaningful teamwork across everybody involved in the payment process and (b) comprehensive practice management infrastructure that matches in power the payer's infrastructure.

The Vericle Billing System is based on creating the "network effect" by following two strategies:

1. Match the payer's billing knowledge with an aggregated, shared knowledge base.
2. Match the payer's processing capacity with an integrated, comprehensive infrastructure.

Strategy 1: Match the Payer's Billing Knowledge with an Aggregated, Shared Knowledge Base

Over the past two decades, the payers have allocated huge resources to perfect their systems. Only meaningful teamwork is effective in matching payers' methodologies to keep your money away from you. Your biller must be able to establish and maintain disciplined teamwork in two important ways:

- **Interprovider teamwork** – Consolidate payment monitoring to accumulate the big picture of the payer's performance. Share every claims processing improvement across all providers. Enable economies of scale—the larger the network of providers using this approach, the greater and more frequent are the opportunities to get the payers to pay the money they owe you.

- **Provider-biller teamwork** – An effective and accountable communication system expedites the exchange of information and claim reprocessing. Without such a system, billers may find themselves fighting both payer and provider for missing information. Make the payment process 100% transparent to all involved. Log and communicate every action taken to get the claim paid. Establish a zero-tolerance environment for finger-pointing—we're all in the same boat.

Strategy 2: Match the Payer's Processing Capacity with an Integrated, Comprehensive Infrastructure

Your system must integrate and leverage information for four goals: payer's-side automation, audit risk management, patient relationship management, and practice workflow management.

- **Automate the payer's side of the claim flow.** Industry insiders call this connection between two different systems a "handshake." Claims stop spending time shuttling back and forth between payers and providers—so they get paid sooner and, ultimately, more often. Systems include on-demand reports to calculate reconciliations, automatically discover problematic claims, and allow continuous discovery and addition of claims processing rules to match the payer's system.

- **Reduce audit risk – Avoid audit threat by preparing for an audit.** Integrate disciplined visit documentation procedures using SOAP notes. Monitor and red-flag claims for audit trigger potential in real time. Track claims that might offend national or local frequencies for specific CPT codes.

- **Build patient relationships and actively maintain patient loyalty.** Focus on targeted patient attraction and loyalty development. Provide individual, timely, and meaningful information. Avoid billing confusions or errors.

- **Eliminate waste – Integrate the front and back office with centralized practice workflow management.** Integrated scheduling and billing functionality helps avoid unbillable encounters, while integrated EMR/SOAP notes and billing helps maintain compliance, readiness for post-payment audit, and penalty avoidance. An integrated system enables automated tracking of compliance and red-flagging of audit risk.

Chapter 7

The Network Effect

People handle adversity differently, and some break down sooner than others. When a team that's focused on a common goal faces adverse conditions, dissent among some of the team members precludes them from reaching a shared goal. Under extreme conditions, a mutiny isn't just mission-critical—it can leave everybody dead. The famous explorer Ernest Shackleton, best remembered for his Antarctic expedition of 1914–1916 in the ship Endurance, managed such risks by assigning the whiny, complaining crew members to sleep in his own tent and share the chores with him. Clustering the "complainers" with him minimized their negative influence on others, and this helped his team survive and accomplish their goals.

In the payer-provider conflict, the providers who accept lower reimbursement, and who don't challenge underpayments or delayed payments, make it easier for the payers to maintain their market control (oligopsony). Vericle's network helps providers maintain their payment schedules and motivation by establishing a shared discipline for clients and billers alike, in terms of both thought and action.

In *Good to Great*, Jim Collins articulates a management methodology that's based on a process of buildup followed by breakthrough.

This can be broken into three broad stages, each driven by three key concepts:

1. Disciplined people – Level 5 leadership, and "first who . . . then what"
2. Disciplined thought – Confrontation of the brutal facts (yet without losing faith) and the "hedgehog" concept (simplicity within the "three circles")
3. Disciplined action – A culture of discipline and technology accelerators

Wrapping around this entire framework is a concept of "flywheel"—which, under disciplined people, thought, and action, accumulates inertia and takes the company from good to great.

One concept in *Good to Great* methodology is called The Stockdale Paradox. It's named after Admiral Jim Stockdale, who was imprisoned in Vietnam and repeatedly tortured over eight years. In a conversation with Collins, Stockdale described how he survived while so many died after just months in captivity:

> "I never lost faith in the end of the story. I never doubted not only that I would get out, but also that I would prevail in the end and turn the experience into the defining event of my life, which, in retrospect, I would not trade."
>
> "Who didn't make it out?" asked Collins.
>
> "The optimists," replied Stockdale. "They were the ones who said 'we're going to be out by Christmas.' And, Christmas would come and Christmas would go. Then they'd say, 'We're going to be out by Easter.' And Easter would come, and Easter would go. And then Thanksgiving, and then it would be Christmas again. Then they died of a broken heart.
>
> "You must never confuse faith that you will prevail in the

> end—which you can never afford to lose—with the discipline to confront the most brutal facts of your current reality, whatever they might be," says Stockdale.[51]

Holding those two seemingly contradictory notions in his head simultaneously was the key to Stockdale surviving. And it's a perfect summary of the mindset you need to manage your office billing. You have to believe that you'll be paid for your work. But you can never let your belief cloud your perception of reality: the payments to providers are costs for payers, whose objective is to improve profitability for their shareholders and, therefore, to reduce their payments to providers.

Claims are not paid by waiting for the payers to pay them. Claims are paid by payers who discover that delay and underpayment are more expensive than payment in full and on time (see Chapter 3). Without a system to make the payers pay, you'll default to the payer's system and find yourself giving up control.

Vericle is a system that can help make the payers pay—and it leverages the "network effect" to amplify its value. The network effect, according to Wikipedia, "causes a good or service to have a value to a potential customer which depends on the number of other customers who own the good or are users of the service."[52] One consequence of a network effect is that the purchase of a service by one individual indirectly benefits others who also use the same service. For example, by purchasing a telephone, a person makes other telephones more useful. The resulting bandwagon effect is a positive feedback loop.

For Vericle, the network effect (also known as Metcalfe's law) says that while Vericle's costs are proportional to the number of submitted claims, the value of Vericle is proportional to the *square* of the number

[51] Collins, *Good to Great.*

[52] Wikipedia, *Network Effect.*

of practice owners using it. For example, if you multiply the number of Vericle's users by 10, your systemwide cost goes up by a factor of 10, but the value goes up a hundredfold. In other words, Metcalfe's law, as applied to Vericle, says that the value of Vericle to the individual practice owner is proportional to the number, n, of other practice owners who share the same billing knowledge base and processes. Now, multiply this value by the number of practice owners, and you have a value for the whole operation that's roughly proportional to n^2 (Figure 9).

Figure 9. Vericle's Network Effect

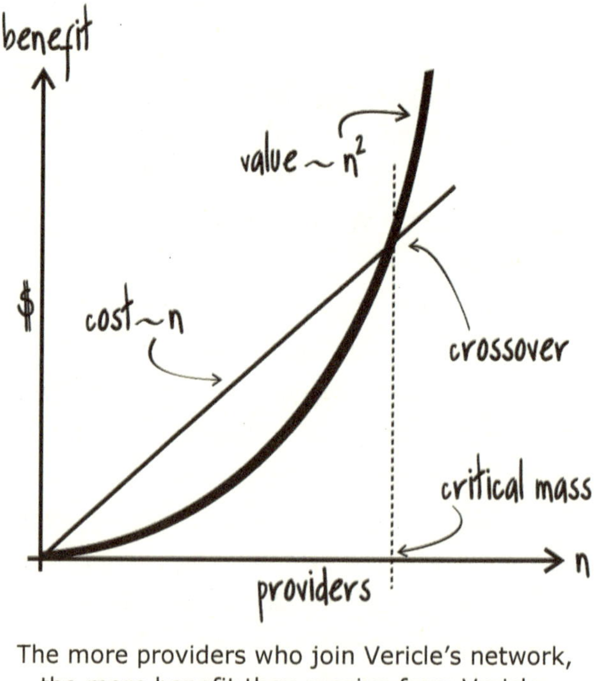

The more providers who join Vericle's network, the more benefit they receive from Vericle.

In the early 1980s, when Robert Metcalfe discovered his law, he was vague about "value." In those days, it had something to do with sharing expensive resources (like fax machines and printers), exchanging electronic mail, and accessing communications technologies (such as the Internet).

For Vericle users, value is defined in four ways: improved collections, lower audit risk, efficient practice management, and added revenue sources. And, according to Metcalfe's law, this value continues to grow, in step with each newly joining practice, long after you started using Vericle's system (Figure 10).

Figure 10. Vericle Levels the Playing Field for Providers

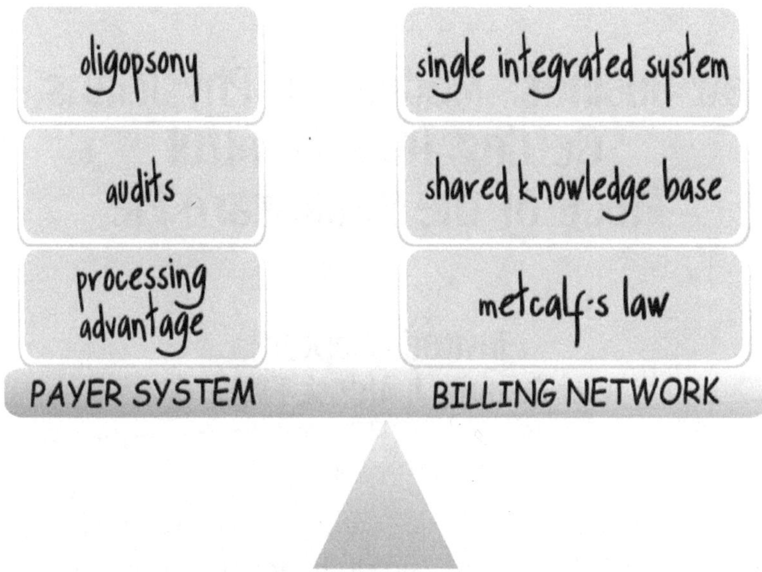

The billing network allows the providers to consolidate their processing volumes and resources, matching the payer's billing processing performance and controlling the billing process.

Chapter 8

New Business Models for Physicians – Getting Their Rightful "Piece of the Healthcare Pie"

Invited Chapter
Dennis J. Alessi, Esq.

For decades, the piece of the healthcare dollar received by physicians has shrunk, and the trend clearly appears to be continuing in that direction. Insurance carriers are paying less for out-of-network services, causing patients to pay a larger portion of the fees as their co-insurance obligation—and possibly forcing these patients to seek the services of in-network physicians in the future. Carriers are reducing reimbursement levels to participating providers, and they're engaging in guerilla warfare in the claims/reimbursement process to further forestall and reduce what they pay physicians for their services. Medicare reimbursement levels are a political football almost every year. Currently, for some services, reimbursements are less than the physicians' costs to provide them.

How have physicians reacted to this situation? Some simply work longer hours, see more patients, and cut to the bone operating expenses and other overhead costs. Others, where practicable, have gone out of network; still others do not accept insurance at all. None of these are long-term solutions.

First, physicians can work only so many hours, and see so many patients, before quality of care suffers.

Second, our experience is that, with the current business model that generally prevails—small group practices with four or five physician members—the economies that can be realized are limited, and most practices reached these limits long ago.

Third, the New Jersey Department of Banking and Insurance (DOBI) has already proposed regulations to limit, to a multiplier of Medicare reimbursement levels, how much out-of-network physicians can charge. While this attempt was beaten back last year by the Medical Society of New Jersey, you can be certain that the insurance carriers will try again. The Board of Medical Examiners (BME) recently proposed two different sets of regulations that would make it more difficult for surgeons to participate in ambulatory surgery centers—and more difficult for them to obtain nonphysician investors and financing for these centers. These proposed regulations are being fought. The Board has also proposed additional regulations that would further restrict the ability of physicians to establish multidiscipline practices with other healthcare professionals (e.g., nurse practitioners, chiropractors, podiatrists, physical therapists, and the like).

In the end, the insurance carriers have more money, more lobbyists, more political clout, and more staying power than organized medicine in the political and regulatory arenas. Consequently, these are not the arenas that hold long-term prospects for the economic well-being and clinical autonomy of physicians. Also, every time physicians find an avenue to enhance their finances, the carriers seek to close it off. Examples are the proposed DOBI "caps" on out-of-network fees and the BME-proposed restrictions on physicians in ambulatory surgery centers.

We're satisfied that only by enhancing the economic clout of physicians can the trend of lower reimbursement levels be permanently reversed over the long term—while maintaining, and even improving, the quality and efficiency of care. When physicians are properly organized into larger "Super Groups," which they control and which are sensitive to their needs for collegiality, they're able to do the following:

1. Effect significant economies and efficiencies.
2. Negotiate higher reimbursement levels with insurance carriers.
3. Maintain, and even improve, the quality of care.
4. Maintain clinical autonomy and the atmosphere of a small group practice.

A Super Group can be structured in two different practice models. One is horizontal integration. This is when a fairly large number of physicians all in one specialty—such as urology, gastroenterology, or cardiology—within a geographic area form one group. With so many physicians in one specialty and one practice, they can negotiate higher reimbursement levels because they have command of such a large share of the market for their specialty services within their geographic area.

Vertical integration is when a core group of internists or family practitioners create a single practice together, along with a number of different specialty physicians to whom these primary care physicians most often refer their patients. For example, a group of internists may find that their most frequent referral is to a cardiologist, so they hire a part-time cardiologist for their practice. Then they continue to build a multispecialty practice around this core of primary care physicians, who refer their patients to the various specialty physicians, all within their one Super Group practice. In this model, the Super Group is built more slowly over time, in layers. Part-time, and then full-time, specialty physicians, in different specialties, are added as the core of primary care physicians also increases. In turn, this increases the numbers and types of referrals they can make within the Super Group to a larger, increasingly diverse set of specialty physicians.

Once the Super Group reaches a certain volume of patients, it can then begin hiring—even on a part-time basis, initially—other allied healthcare professionals and technicians, such as physician assistants, nurse practitioners, physical therapists, various technicians, and the like. These individuals are all on salary and don't have an ownership interest in the Super Group. Accordingly, these allied healthcare professionals and technicians become profit makers for the Super Group, and the profits are another source of income for the physician owners.

There are also two different facility models for a Super Group. One is to house all of the Super Group's physicians in one physical location. Obviously, this results in the greatest economies and efficiencies of operations. However, it's not always feasible, or necessarily desirable, in a suburban setting where the Super Group wants to solicit patients from a larger geographic area. The other facility model is to have a number of satellite offices, like spokes on a wheel, for a large geographic circumference. This model is less efficient because of the multiple facilities, but economies can still be obtained from centralized billing and other support services. There's also the benefit of each office maintaining its prior atmosphere of a small group practice.

Conclusion

Admittedly, there are healthcare regulatory, antitrust, and other legal issues—and still other business and personality hurdles—that must be overcome to create a "Super Group." However, it's already been done in New Jersey, and we can replicate it elsewhere. We're satisfied that, going forward, only such Super Groups can restore to physicians the rightful compensation they deserve and the clinical autonomy to which they're entitled as plenary license holders.

About the Author

Dennis J. Alessi, Esq., is a director at Mandelbaum, Salsburg, Gold, Lazris & Discenza, PC, co-chairman of its Health Care Law Department, and its lead attorney for representing clients in the healthcare industry. Mr. Alessi's expertise spans structuring healthcare businesses and transactions, advising clients on compliance, arbitrating disputes between healthcare entities or individual providers, and litigating healthcare-related issues in federal and state courts. Mr. Alessi received a BA from the College of William and Mary in 1971, a JD from the New England School of Law in 1976, and an LLM with honors from New York University in 1980. He is admitted to practice before the bars of New York, New Jersey, and the District of Columbia.

Part II

Workflow Processes

If you don't know where you are going, any road will take you there.

—Cheshire Cat
Alice's Adventures in Wonderland
Lewis Carroll

Network effect becomes meaningful after reaching a certain "critical mass" of knowledge—which, in turn, requires a "critical mass" of practices to begin using Vericle. At the critical mass point, the value obtained from the service is greater than the price paid for it.

Four factors determine Vericle's value: efficient operations, improved collections, reduced audit risk, and added sources of revenue. Efficient operations provide value to practice owners prior to reaching critical mass.

Vericle brings efficiency using workflow technology. Workflow management technologies play two central roles in Vericle—first, for managing patient flow, and second, for billing process flow. While the two flows differ in terms of participants, expected actions, results, and exceptions, both flows capitalize on automation and exception handling.

Accordingly, Part II starts with a chapter introducing the concepts of Straight-Through Billing and Transparency. Chapter 10 lists criteria for evaluating billing software and office management solutions. Chapter 11 discusses computer-aided patient scheduling. Chapter 12 continues to focus on billing performance by considering over-the-counter (OTC) payment problems and solutions. Centralized billing workflow and the characteristic Vericle workbench are discussed in Chapter 13. Chapter 14 reviews computer-aided coding concepts. Finally, Chapter 15 presents a formal problem-tracking process and the underlying technology to bridge a medical practice with an outsourced billing service provider.

Chapter 9

Straight-Through Billing

Medical billing complexity and massive volumes of daily claims render manual claims processes incapable of protecting both the provider and the payer from underpayments, overpayments, and billing compliance violations. Straight-Through Billing (STB) addresses complexity and volume processing problems by automating the majority of the claim flow and focusing the billing follow-up specialists on exceptions only. An STB process flags problems, routes them for follow-up, and enables online correction and resubmission. STB methodology implements billing service transparency and focuses management on strategic process improvement opportunities.

Straight-Through Billing integrates the billing process into the practice management workflow, automates the vast majority of transactions, focuses manual labor on exceptions, and establishes a process for continuous improvement.

Practice Management Integration

First, integrated practice management and billing workflow connects patient scheduling, medical record management, and billing into a single process. Every participant of the practice management workflow receives a unified and coherent picture of practice workload, patient and provider location, resource availability, and cash flow.

Transaction Automation

Transaction automation streamlines and expedites the billing process by automating claim validation, payer message reconciliation, and billing workflow management:

- Automated claim validation eliminates errors downstream and reduces processing time because it flags errors before submitting the claim to the payer.
- Automated claim message reconciliation eliminates the costly search for the original claim and standardizes message communication, further eliminating the need to decipher the (often cryptic) payer's message.
- Automated billing workflow management drives the follow-up discipline required for the resolution of claim denial and underpayment incidents, and it establishes a high degree of process transparency for all billing process participants, resulting in full and timely payments.

Focus on Exceptions

Focusing manual labor on exceptions requires timely exception identification, routing to follow-up personnel, online error correction, and rigorous follow-up tracking. Again, process transparency, as implemented in Vericle-like systems, enables tracking exception follow-up.

Continuous Process Improvement

Finally, a process for continuous improvement requires continuous observability of every process attribute and a modification methodology for both automated claim processing and manual exception follow-up tracking.

Straight-Through Billing implements billing transparency by design, because billing transparency is an integral attribute of every component of the STB process.

Straight-Through Billing Architecture

The Straight-Through Billing systems architecture mirrors the architecture of general Straight-Through Processing (STP) systems developed for the financial services industry. Such systems require effective workflow management, a knowledge-based validation system, connectivity to all process participants (including online data reconciliation), and tracking of problem resolution. Therefore, a typical Vericle-like STB system has a three-tiered architecture:

- Back-end processing engine, designed for a high-volume transaction processing environment
- Middle tier, using Java Servlet technology
- Front end, using an HTML-JavaScript, zero-footprint client

An STB system (e.g., Vericle) based on the methodology outlined here implements rich functionality, which allows the following to be automated:

- Computer-aided preferential patient scheduling
- Integrated electronic medical records

- Online computer-aided coding
- Real-time claim validation and patient eligibility testing
- Electronic claim submission
- Payment posting, reconciliation, and verification of meeting contractual obligations
- Monitoring of audit risk and billing compliance
- Tracking of denial appeal process

Quantitative STB Management

Straight-Through Billing methodology allows for quantitative management, since the likelihood of the entire process failing can be estimated as the product of such items for each individual workflow step. A Vericle-like STB system tracks the percentage of clean claims (claims paid in full, and within the allocated time frame, without any manual intervention) and focuses the management on those process aspects that yield the greatest potential improvement. Thus, STB methodology focuses on exceptions at both the tactical and strategic management levels.

Chapter 10

Practice Perfect – 10 Criteria for the Best Billing Software and Office Management Solution

Medical practice IT must meet five functional criteria and five technology criteria:

1. **Clinical relevance** – Technology can help the healing process only if it helps make treatment decisions at the point of care. Therefore, it must be available next to the treatment table, and it must have an intuitive user interface to facilitate simple data entry and help online reporting.

2. **Patient relationship management** – Successful practice development requires perfectly managed patient relationships, starting with establishing and tracking financial care plans, appointment reminders, balance follow-ups, and avoiding unbillable appointments.

3. **Compliant SOAP notes** – SOAP is short for Subjective,

Objective, Assessment, and Plan:

- **Subjective** describes the patient's current condition, including all pertinent and negative symptoms. Document how symptoms impact activities of daily living. Use the standard SOAP format, modified to SOAAP by adding an extra "A" for Activities of Daily Living.
- **Objective** includes vital signs, findings from physical examinations, and results from laboratory tests. Document functional measurements (e.g., range of motion), comparison data, test results, co-morbidities, etc., to paint a picture of what's going on with the patient.
- **Assessment** is a quick summary of the patient with the main symptoms and diagnosis, including a differential diagnosis and a list of other possible diagnoses (usually in the order of most likely to least likely).
- **Plan** is what the healthcare provider will do to treat the patient's concerns. This should address each item of the differential diagnosis. Document goals for the patient, and establish a reasonable timeline to reach those goals. Document the patient's progress toward those goals in the daily SOAAP notes.

4. **Full and timely payments** – Revenue-cycle management software must help the practice manager make sure that every service encounter gets paid in full and on time. It must provide a full and detailed 24/7 account of all actions on every claim, systematic discovery of denials, patient invoicing, electronic claims submissions to payers, payment posting and reconciliation with charges, HIPAA compli-

ance, built-in tests for medical necessity, and comprehensive online reporting.

5. **Audit risk management** – This consists of continuous monitoring for potential compliance violations and meticulous management of patient encounter notes.

6. **Reporting and transparency** – Without transparency, billing may not be reliable. To observe every step of the billing process on a continuous 24/7 basis, reporting must be available using a secure HIPAA-compliant connection over the Internet. Vendors that manage their own billing technology typically have better control of reporting capabilities in terms of scope, analysis, frequency, and transparency. At the minimum, the following features must be available:
   - **Operational report** – Showing total claims and dollar amounts submitted, paid, adjusted, written off, and failed. It allows breakdown by CPT, payer, referral, or any combination thereof.
   - **Denials report** – Showing the list of denied claims and a log of follow-up actions. If you sort it by amount paid, you can determine the smallest payment that the billing service will fight for.
   - **Compliance report** – Showing the potential for post-payment audit and itemizing compliance violations.

   Reports must allow arbitrary data aggregation and drill-in. Exporting to Excel spreadsheets for further analysis is a very useful feature.

7. **Billing quality metric** – Make a list of metrics available

online. Focus on collections completeness and payment delay. Can the system report the differences between payers and between various CPT codes in real time? What is the denial follow-up success rate?

8. **Data entry protocols** – Modern technologies allow the doctor to take over coding and reduce the billing role to claims processing and follow-up. A technology-competent vendor will supply your "superbill" online, along with a separate form for patient and charge entry, EOB posting, and online claim editing. Similarly, much of data entry validity, including some claim scrubbing, will be done online at the point of data entry.

9. **ASP or SaaS delivery model** – Rapid technology progress results in a low return on investment in software licenses, typical of client-server technology. Therefore, monthly leasing arrangements with zero up-front investment, typical of ASP (application service provider) or SaaS (Software as a Service) delivery models are preferable to license purchase.

10. **Data security and protection** – Review data center facilities. Ask for evidence on HIPAA compliance; claims must be viewed only on a "need to know" basis, and access to claims and modifications must be thoroughly documented. Data must be protected with redundant disaster recovery measures. Review backup processes, backup intervals, and data restore capabilities.

Summary

Increasing regulatory scrutiny, poor in-house billing performance, and rapid technology progress are key growth drivers in medical information technology. On one hand, thousands of outsourced billing solutions and software vendors ensure continued competitiveness in terms of both service quality and pricing. On the other hand, the lack of standards and uniform metrics among the vendors, combined with their large numbers, frustrates the selection process. Ten effective guidelines will streamline your outsourced solution selection process and reduce the costs of switching vendors.

Chapter 11

Computer-aided Patient Scheduling

Without a computerized scheduler, a practice has a less than 2% chance to earn the title of a "better performing practice," according to the Medical Group Management Association.[53] A massive investment in scheduling features across a wide spectrum of billing products is another indication of the importance of computerized scheduling.

Convenience and front office efficiencies are two obvious benefits of a computerized scheduling system; without them, the only manual way to find out if a specific patient has a scheduled appointment is to flip through the appointment book page by page. Worse, manual scheduling hurts both patient satisfaction and practice financial performance because of scheduling inconsistencies and unbilled (and therefore unpaid) visits.

But the benefits of integrated computerized scheduling stretch far beyond convenience, front office efficiencies, and better charge follow-up of stand-alone, albeit computerized, scheduling. A well-designed and integrated scheduler allows preferential patient scheduling, which,

[53] Medical Group Management Association, *Performance and Practices.*

along with improved controls, helps revenue optimization and practice compliance. Next, we review key aspects of computerized scheduling, and we demonstrate important benefits of integrated scheduling, billing, and compliance management.

Scheduling Policies

Computerized schedulers allow a combination of single- or multiple-interval scheduling, with open-access scheduling subject to various priority constraints. Such priority-constraint-driven, open-access scheduling creates preferential appointments based on patient demographics or insurance coverage.

Single-interval scheduling allocates appointments at regular intervals—every 5 to 15 minutes, depending on the specialty. The downside of single-interval scheduling is that as soon as one appointment takes longer than the allocated slot, all subsequent patients have to wait.

Multiple-interval scheduling also sets appointments at regular intervals—however, unlike single-interval scheduling, it allocates the length of the appointment depending on the chief complaint. Such scheduling requires up-front categorization of key appointment types and their projected lengths. For instance, an initial appointment might take 30 minutes, while a routine injection might take only 5 minutes.

Open-access scheduling requires holding open several appointments every day. These open appointments are filled only within 48 hours of the appointment, catering to same-day or last-minute patient requests. Open-access scheduling improves access to the physician, reduces no-shows, and eliminates patient screening time. The downside of open-access scheduling is, of course, the potential for longer patient waiting lines or physician idle time because of the inability to maintain a predictable patient flow.

One way to balance practice workload is to schedule group, routine, or repeat appointments during slow hours. For instance, pediatric well-child visits or patients with a particular chronic disease—such as congestive heart failure or diabetes—could be scheduled for early mornings, when there are typically fewer patients waiting in line. These scheduled visits include educational components and often involve multidisciplinary teams. Patients also benefit from the socialization aspect of group visits; members encourage one another, exercise together, and so forth. A good scheduler allows a repeat appointment schedule subject to total frequency and time slot constraints.

Compliance Process

An integrated scheduler verifies the filing of a signed patient consent form—and, in certain cases, a signed ABN form. An ABN (Advance Beneficiary Notice) serves three goals:

- To protect the beneficiaries from liability for services denied as not reasonable (depends on the frequency or duration) and necessary (depends on the diagnosis and the provider's specialty)
- To protect the provider's revenue by shifting financial liability for denied services to the patient
- To provide documentation for a Medicare audit

For more complex procedures, the scheduler warns the front office about the need to obtain up front all of the required diagnostic test results and clearances.

Billing Interface

The integrated scheduler avoids unbillable patient encounters and reconciles visits with patient balances. It checks outstanding patient balances and verifies coverage and eligibility at the point of scheduling, prior to the appointment. In many cases, such a test discovers data entry errors too, reducing the payment cycle at later stages.

Additionally, the insurance company may require referrals or separate pre-authorization/certification for certain procedures, refusing the payment if the procedure was performed without a referral or pre-authorization. The integrated scheduler has access to medical records to supply necessary background and diagnosis information to obtain pre-authorization. Finally, without the ability to reconcile visits with payments, the practice owner cannot be sure that every visit resulted in a payment.

Practice Flow Interface

The integrated scheduler manages the entire patient flow, providing continuously updated arrival lists, checkoffs, and office/room tracking. Further, the scheduler tracks no-shows and follow-up actions. Detailed reports include daily schedules, load reports, missed appointments, free time, canceled appointments, etc.

Patient Interface

Advanced schedulers include appointment reminders and provide online registration and online scheduling request forms. Online scheduling request forms must take into account the risk of scheduling patients beyond the scope of the practice, which a live operator would have screened out.

Summary

Traditional stand-alone scheduling systems reduce idle time for employees, lower provider frustration, and reduce patient waiting time. Modern integrated schedulers accomplish more ambitious goals of increasing revenue, reducing administrative costs, and shortening billing cycles. An integrated scheduler handles multiple providers, locations, scheduling policies, and patient preparation processes, and it has bi-directional compliance and billing interfaces. Most importantly, an integrated scheduler implements a consistent preferential scheduling policy.

Chapter 12

Over-the-Counter Payment Performance

For many practices, the proportion of over-the-counter (OTC) payments has recently grown from an average of 15% to as high as 75% of total payments.[54] Systematic OTC collections, including a measurable process that emphasizes up-front collections, often yield double-digit billing performance improvement. Most importantly, a disciplined and transparent collections process improves provider-patient communications, while early payment collections are also quicker and easier. Better communications and happier patients mean better health and a more profitable practice.

OTC payments include co-pays, fees for noncovered elective services or retail products, and any outstanding balances. Successful collections of OTC payments require a measurable collections process, a specialized information technology infrastructure, and adequate personnel training and discipline.

OTC payment collection performance and costs greatly depend on the elapsed time between service and payment. The dependence of collection performance on timing stems from the dynamic nature of the

[54] Capko, "Physicians Practice Pearls."

price-value relation. Initially, perception of value received is high in the patient's mind. Similarly, the correlation between value and price is also high. However, OTC payment collections become more difficult as the patient's memory of that value fades.

Systematic measurement of OTC payment quality is critical for its performance improvement. Vericle's OTC payment quality metrics include the percentage of accounts receivable beyond 120 days and the time spent on collecting old account balances. While the national average of the first metric hovers around 18%, our experience shows that some practices may accumulate as much as 50% of their accounts receivable beyond 120 days. The second metric measures the front office collections efficiency, and it also varies widely—from a few hours per month to double-digit hours per week spent by front office personnel chasing unpaid OTC invoices.

According to Vericle experience, the following systematic and measurable payment collections process leverages electronic medical billing software and establishes the discipline required for double-digit billing collections improvement:

1. **Publish your payment collections policy** and standard responses to typical patient objections.

2. **Clarify patient statements** generated by your electronic medical billing software.
    a. Make outstanding balances easily identifiable.
    b. Add specific language about the time period expected for payment of the balance due (typically upon service or product delivery).
    c. Include a phone number for patients to call with questions.

3. **Use electronic medical billing software** to do the fol-

lowing:

   a. Test a patient's eligibility and coverage (the results of such a test define a patient's co-pay prior to arrival at the clinic).
   b. Generate front office alerts about an impending visit by a patient with an unpaid OTC balance.

4. **Train clinic physicians** to direct patients to front office staff to review financial statements.

5. **Train your front office** to collect OTC payments.
   a. Hold your front office staff accountable by setting up specific and personal collection goals.
   b. Use electronic medical billing software to track collections performance by individual front office staff.
   c. Establish personal awards for accomplishing collections goals, and periodically review personal collections performance.
   d. Train your office staff to receive electronic medical billing software alerts.
   e. Develop a payment collections script and rehearse it with front office staff to improve staff-patient communications.

Summary

Successful OTC payment collections help patient relationship management and improve practice profitability. They require a measurable collections process, a specialized information technology infrastructure, and adequate personnel training and discipline.

Chapter 13

Centralized Billing Workflow

Reducing accounts receivable is a key responsibility of the billing function in a medical practice. This chapter compares traditional (distributed) billing functions with centralized workflow management. It shows that centralized workflow management yields significant advantages over the distributed approach in terms of the ability to manage accounts receivable. However, it also requires significant investments in process, technology, and personnel training.

Benefits

Centralized workflow management is superior to traditional billing operations management because it enables continuous billing process improvements and helps avoid the repetition of errors while reducing the dependency on specific individual billing knowledge. The billing process improves systematically along the key performance dimensions, including the amount and timeliness of the payment.

Centralized workflow management accomplishes such important benefits using a two-pronged approach that's based on (a) formal encoding of billing and compliance knowledge and (b) a computer program to apply the knowledge and manage claim follow-up lists.

As an encoded billing knowledge base grows, the accuracy of the claims and the speed of the process increases. Additionally, the staff can spend more time focusing on exceptions, while an increasing majority of claims are processed automatically.

Moreover, a centralized workflow shares its billing rules across all providers and billers. Therefore, errors discovered and corrected for one provider will be avoided in the future for all of the providers using the system.

Workflow

Workflow is defined as a sequence of actions performed on a claim until it is paid. Centralized workflow management must quickly separate "clean" claims from potential failures, submit clean claims to payers, and flag potential failures for correction. Workflow must also track the correction process, ensuring its integration with other sources of failures and its successful completion. Finally, workflow must facilitate meticulous documentation of every step to enable continuous improvement and learning from experience.

Failed Claim

A failed claim is a claim that's flagged by the workflow system up front as invalid, rejected by the payer after submission, or not properly adjudicated within 30 days—in other words, a claim that requires follow-up.

Workbench

Centralized workflow manages follow-up lists of failed claims using workbenches. A workbench is a list of failed claims assigned to an individual biller or operator. Such an individual assignment of work enables continuous and individual performance tracking and improvement.

Activity Triggers

In a medical billing operation, the follow-up lists and to-do lists of individual actions for each failed claim constantly change. To manage multiple to-do lists, the centralized workflow system has activity triggers. Activity triggers are the heart of task automation; they help determine what's important. Activity triggers match up promises with events, and they manage individual work queues in the process.

In order to remember to call a payer or provider weeks after the phone conversation in which a payment or claim clarification was promised, a billing clerk must sort through a call-on-receipt folder several times a day. Activity triggers eliminate the reliance on personal memory and enable communication between individual workbenches. They are the strings that tie billing activities together. For example, when Mary from the provider's office updates the claim with the correct ICD-9, the system needs to be aware that the claim is ready for validation—and John in the billing office needs to know, so that he can review it again to see if the validation failed or to schedule its transmission to the payer.

Task Automation

Centralized workflow eliminates paper-based steps. Like a relay team passing the baton, the billing staff members electronically pass along their work without delays. Instead of printing, faxing, and following up with an email or a phone call, all tasks arrive complete with supporting documentation. Rather than thumbing through reams of paper and reading scribbled notes, billers receive on-screen reminders when tasks are due.

Process Monitoring

Centralized workflow also simplifies process monitoring. Providers and managers use dashboards to review key indicators. Like activity triggers, dashboards help focus personnel on what's important from a high-level perspective. They show key business information that tells us if we're paid more or less over time, if our charges are going up or down, and if our follow-up policies are too lenient. They tell us whether we're heading in the right direction and act like lighthouses to keep us off the shoals. When we see that warning light, we can drill into the details and take corrective action.

Summary

The key difference between Vericle-like centralized workflow management and traditional approaches is that a centralized workflow guides the operator to identify claims that need follow-up. There's no need to manually look up reports to analyze data and select claims for follow-up. A Vericle-like approach ensures follow-up consistency and timeliness.

Chapter 14

Computer-aided Coding

The average practice submits half of its codes wrong, while some practices rarely exceed more than one correct code out of every five. Inexact and inconsistent coding increases the risks of undercharging, overcharging, and post-payment audit. This chapter outlines the evolution of coding from an individualistic art toward a disciplined and systematic process.

It's convenient to review the role of coding in the context of the entire claim processing cycle: patient appointment scheduling, pre-authorization, patient encounter note creation, charge generation, claim scrubbing, claim submission to payer, and follow-up—which, in turn, includes denial or underpayment identification, payment reconciliation, and appeal management. The importance of thorough knowledge and the correct application of coding rules at the charge generation stage of the claim processing cycle are well known and have been frequently discussed. Less obvious, but no less important, is the ability to make correct interpretations of the same rules at the claim follow-up stage during denial or underpayment analysis and upon receiving the payment and explanation of benefits.

Coding is difficult because of a four-dimensional complexity. First, the sheer volume and intricacy of coding rules makes it difficult to select the right procedure code, correct modifier, and necessary diagnosis code for the given medical note. For instance, a claim will be denied if you charged for two CPT codes but provided an ICD-9 code that shows medical necessity for only one CPT code. Next, the payer-specific modifications exacerbate the complexity of coding, creating the need to code or process the same procedures differently, depending on the payer. For example, some payers require medical notes attached to some CPT codes in addition to standard ICD-9 codes. Third, the codes and regulations change over time, necessitating continuous coding education and re-education. Finally, charge generation and claim follow-up are disconnected in space and time, and since different people often perform these tasks, such performance disparities add to the confusion and costs of the claim processing cycle.

Only experienced coders can handle such complexity, but experience too often turns into a handicap. For example, in the absence of a reliable self-correcting process, the coder or the follow-up person may make the same mistake over and over. Hence, ad hoc coding is error-prone and expensive. Paper superbill-driven coding improves upon traditional coding because it allows fewer errors and eliminates some of the costs. Computer-aided coding with an integrated superbill completes the transformation of coding from an individualistic art to a disciplined and systematic process, and it's the most reliable and least expensive solution.

Traditional Coding

Since the practice owner is ultimately responsible for coding quality, it behooves the physician to personally manage the coding process. But traditionally, in the absence of systematic practice management, the physician looked for a way to avoid the burden of coding. Such an approach to coding is both error-prone and expensive. The average error rate for CPT coding is 45%–55% (Figure 11).[55] Some specialties (e.g., interventional radiologists) have trouble exceeding even 18% of correct coding.[56]

Figure 11. Billing Error Distribution

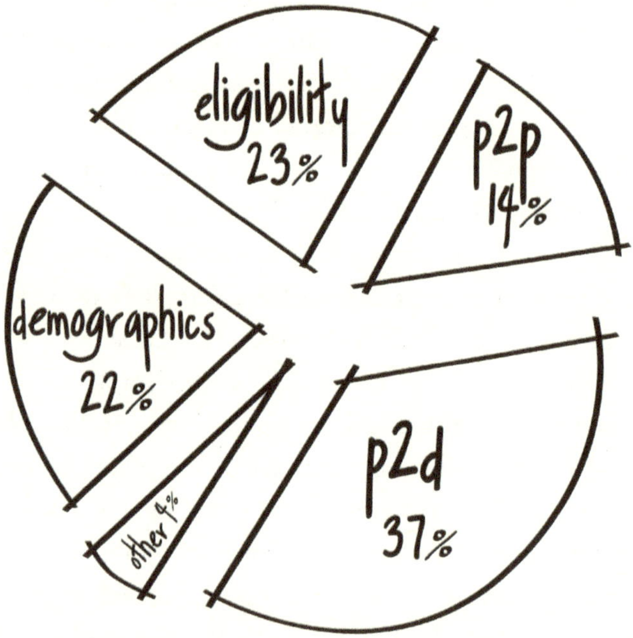

Medical necessity (Procedure to Diagnosis "P2D" and Procedure to Procedure "P2P") make up more than half of the errors.[57]

Traditional coding involves the doctor, data entry personnel, and a certified coder. The doctor dictates, types, or handwrites descriptions of diagnoses and procedures, without listing actual codes. The data entry personnel enter codes based on reading the doctor's descriptions, and the certified coder supervises and audits the quality of coding by

---

[55] Healthcare Financial Management Association, *Tip Sheet.*

[56] Ibid.

[57] Ibid.

the data entry personnel.

The traditional coding process is error-prone because the certified coder does not audit 100% of entered codes and because such a process does not have a vehicle for maintaining context between the charge's creation and the claim's follow-up stages. The errors may become especially expensive upon post-payment audit of the charges by the insurance company. This process is also expensive because multiple people are involved in the coding process and because the errors, if discovered at all, will be discovered only downstream, raising the costs of error correction.

Paper Superbill-driven Coding

A pre-compiled, superbill-driven coding process places the doctor in control of coding, ties together claim creation and follow-up stages, and avoids many shortcomings of traditional coding. Such a process delivers the twofold advantage of lower cost and improved communication. First, the doctor personally codes at the end of the patient encounter, without involving data entry personnel in the middle. Second, the paper superbill serves as a formal vehicle for coding information communication between the charge creation and claim follow-up stages. Additionally, a pre-compiled superbill improves coding consistency across all doctors within the same practice.

This superbill creation process has four stages:

1. List the codes used most often first (use a CPT frequency report for discovery).
2. List the diagnosis codes.
3. Leave room for ancillary services.
4. Include the patient's information.

Along with the advantages over the traditional coding process, the paper-based superbill still has four shortcomings. First, the data must be re-entered into the system from the paper superbill, introducing the potential for errors. Next, the superbill must be reviewed periodically to adjust for changes in practice operations. Worse, it's difficult to keep up with changes in coding regulations, necessary modifiers, and bundling decisions that differ across various payers. Finally, the paper superbill contributes nothing to up-front coding error identification and correction, which can delay potential error identification and resolution to post-submission or, even worse, to post-payment phases. Obviously, the later in the process the error is identified, the more expensive its correction.

Computer-aided Coding with Integrated Superbill

Computerization and integration overcome most of the problems of paper superbills. They eliminate duplicate data entry; automate code review and adjustment for frequency, practice operations, and payer idiosyncrasies; and shift much of the error identification and correction from the post-payment stage to the claim pre-submission stage.

Computer-aided coding with an integrated superbill offers multiple advantages:

1. **Dynamic** – Adjusts for changes in practice operations and payer specifics. For instance, it adds an automated alert to satisfy unique payer demands, such as requests for paid drug invoices in addition to an injection CPT code and J code for supplies.
2. **Precise** – Matches codes to EMR, and alerts in real time about potential coding errors—such as confusing modifiers 59, 76, 77, and 91 for repeat procedure or test, or not coding the ICD-9 code to the highest level of possible digits in spite of a specific diagnostic available in EMR.

3. **Defensive** – Allows for real-time profiling of coding patterns to alert about potential audit flags.
4. **Reliable** – Facilitates end-of-day juxtaposition of visits with charges, avoiding unpaid visits.
5. **Inexpensive** – Eliminates the extra data entry step and associated costs, because the doctor can use it directly.

Summary

Coding is a mission-critical responsibility of the practice owner. Computer-aided coding with an integrated superbill places the doctor in control and enables a dynamic, precise, reliable, consistent, defensive, and inexpensive coding process. Superbill digitization and integration overcome the four-dimensional coding complexity; tie it to EMR, patient scheduling, and billing (i.e., to the entire spectrum of practice management functions); and require powerful Vericle-like computing platforms.

Chapter 15

Problem Tracking

Processes involving large volumes of complex billing transactions require effective mechanisms for assigning and tracking problems. Without such mechanisms, billing personnel cannot be held accountable for problem resolution, resulting in a loss of revenue and increased compliance risk. While the medical billing industry has developed specialized systems and processes for the resolution of content problems, little attention has been paid to the methodology for billing process problem resolution. This chapter outlines a process and a technology for resolving integrated billing process problems.

Tracking Methodologies

Medical billing exceptions can be categorized into content and process problems. Content problems have to do with claim content and patterns of processed claims, such as terminology, medical necessity, patient eligibility, denial follow-up, and regulatory billing compliance. Process problems involve claim formatting, system interfaces, entry of patient demographics, posting of charges and payments, printing and mailing/faxing of required information, provider interaction procedures, systems access, and HIPAA compliance.

While streamlining and transparency are important attributes for the resolution of both kinds of problems, the required processes and systems are very different. Content problems tend to be specialized, and they therefore lend themselves to a more structured, almost template-driven solution approach. Process problems, in contrast to content problems, tend to cover a wide variety of knowledge domains, precluding specialization.

The difference in solution methodologies drives the difference in problem tracking. For content problem resolution methodology, please consult the chapters on metrics, Straight-Through Billing, and billing transparency. The remainder of this chapter focuses on process problem tracking.

Billing Process Problem Tracking

A general-purpose tracking system allows for opening a problem ticket, followed by its assignment to specific team member, its reassignment or escalation, its change of status (depending on the problem resolution stage), convenient reporting about sets of tickets in different states or assigned to different team members, and continuous notification of everybody involved about the change of status. Therefore, such a tracking system (e.g., web-based TrackLogix) is constructed around three basic reports, a notification mechanism, and a concept of ticket.

Problem Tracking Reports

These reports show the following:

1. Tickets you owe to others
2. Tickets owed to you

3. Status – a summary table of the team participants with statistics of tickets in different states

Other reports may show and compare individual productivity and responsiveness.

Problem Notification

For transparency, the team members must be continuously aware of every problem resolution status. The simplest way to maintain such awareness is to send an email to every team member about every status change event of a problem ticket. Other popular notification media include paging and short message service (SMS) calls. More sophisticated methods involve selective notification based on the nature of the event or the person assigned to problem resolution.

Problem Ticket

The problem ticket has the following data elements:

1. **Subject** – Short description of the problem

2. **Owner** – Name of the employee responsible for issue resolution

3. **Requestor** – Name of the manager who assigned the issue to the employee

4. **Date** – Date the issue was identified and documented

5. **Scheduled** – Date (time) by which this issue must be resolved

6. **Body** – Detailed issue description

7. **Log** – Time-stamped and owner-stamped history of all documentation, including the following:
    a. Escalation – Issues may be escalated to upper management via TrackLogix by simply changing the owner
    b. Priority change
    c. Status change
    d. Date change
    e. Owner change
    f. Specific action taken to resolve the issue

8. **Priority** – Ranking of issue's importance relative to other issues on the same workbench

9. **Status**
    a. Open for new issue
    b. Pending resolution and waiting for approval
    c. Closed (resolved) and approved

Summary

Vericle-like Straight-Through Billing (STB) systems automate the majority of billing transactions and focus manual follow-up on exceptions. A formal web-based process and problem-tracking system, such as TrackLogix, provides accountability, which is based on a precise account of all process problems and their resolution status. With such a tracking system, all problems are visible to every process participant. An increased level of personal accountability promotes teamwork, increases client satisfaction, and assists in streamlining the process.

$
30
60
90
120

Part III

Metrics, Analysis, and Reporting

It would be so nice if something made sense for a change.

—Alice
Alice's Adventures in Wonderland
Lewis Carroll

Vericle achieves the network effect by combining STP (Straight-Through Processing) methodology with the SaaS (Software as a Service) software delivery method. STP methodology is rooted in the comprehensive measurement of every aspect of the billing process and in continuous process improvement discipline.

Chapter 16 takes us through a critical review of various medical billing performance metrics. Chapter 17 presents an indirect method for analyzing billing performance and understanding the payer-provider dynamics by observing several perspectives of historical "clean claim" data. Chapter 18 introduces the concept of billing transparency and Vericle's dashboard. Chapter 19 discusses the process for structured denial management. Chapter 20 lists the key factors that the practice owner must consider when deciding to participate in or drop a payer's network. The final chapter presents OLAP concepts and second-order SQL queries for lost revenue recovery.

Chapter 16

Service Performance Metrics

Billing performance measurement is an integral part of the medical practice billing process and a prerequisite to effective practice management. Systematic measurement becomes mission-critical with the growth of billing complexity or outsourcing of the billing function. Traditional billing metrics are limited in scope; they focus on the claim submission process, ignoring process imperfections on the insurance (payer) side. Modern computer technologies allow both productive measurement and effective action by the disciplined billing office to improve claim submission and payment processes.

Using appropriate metrics helps improve policies and procedures, shorten revenue cycles, reduce patient complaints, improve financial performance and compliance, increase cash flow, reduce bad debt, identify areas of potential growth, improve employee morale, increase productivity, and reduce costs. Useful metrics must be comprehensive and simple. They must combine both complete end-to-end processes and the individual components of those processes. Metrics must be used consistently over time and must be compared with standards. Obviously, different standards apply to different medical specialties, patient demographics, payers, and samples of CPT codes.

Medical billing metrics typically include compliance, cash balances, charges, accounts receivable, and collection ratios to help monitor cash flow. This chapter focuses on performance metrics.

Collection Ratios

Traditional metrics include gross and net collection ratios. Both metrics are subjective to the individual practice because they compare (often arbitrary) charges with (allowed) payments. (Net collection rate is defined as the ratio of total collections and total charges less adjustments. Gross collection rate is defined as the ratio of total collections to total charges only.) According to the Medical Group Management Association (MGMA) 1998 Cost Survey, adjusted fee-for-service collections (net collections) for family practices in 1997 averaged 98.65%.[58] A declining net collection ratio may be symptomatic of increased contractual write-offs or an insufficient number of denial appeals. This metric is especially useful in the absence of modern computer technology, when it's impossible to compare every payment with the allowed amount, or when the denial appeals process is too expensive. Otherwise, using charges in defining gross and net collection metrics precludes them from the productive discovery of process improvement opportunities.

Days in Accounts Receivable (DAR)

A growing number of days in accounts receivable is symptomatic of a faulty billing process. One way to determine DAR is to count days from the date of service to the date of payment for every claim, and then average that across all claims. A simpler way to compute average number of days in accounts receivable is by taking a ratio of accounts

[58] Medical Group Management Association, *Physician Cost Survey, 1998.*

receivable to average daily charges, or

No. of Days in Accounts Receivable =
(Accounts Receivable / Average Charge) x 365

This metric also depends on the medical specialty, patient demographics, payer mix, and CPT sample. Another downside is that this metric is sensitive to the provider because it counts the lag time of unsubmitted claims for services already delivered. This lag time roughly averages across all payers, making DAR an effective comparison metric between payers for an individual provider, but invalidating it across multiple providers.

One obvious advantage of the DAR metric is its independence of charges. The averaging feature of this metric eliminates sensitivity to a specific day or CPT, but it also hides the behavior shape of the accounts receivable curve.

First-Pass Pay (FPP) Rate and Denial Rate

The FPP rate is the percentage of claims paid in full upon the first submission (subject to federal or state timely payment regulations; most state laws require 15 days for electronic submissions and 30 days for paper submissions).

The denial rate is the complementary metric to the FPP rate. It counts the percentage of claims that require follow-up and therefore cost more to process. Follow-up may take the form of a phone call to the payer to discover a lost claim or to receive interpretation of a denial message, correction of earlier submitted data, resubmission of the original claim, consultation with the provider and medical notes, or denial appeal.

Both FPP and denial rates are very important metrics often used for billing process improvement. The upside of the FPP/denial metric is that it's not affected by the charge, but its downside is that it hides the differences between process imperfections on the claim submission and claim payment sides. To identify patterns of problem CPT codes or payers, the FPP/denial metric needs to be computed and compared across all payer-CPT code pairs, which is a standard feature for modern billing technologies.

Patient Liability

The percentage of patient liability is the ratio of patient responsibility to total billed charges, and it roughly reflects patient deductibles. This metric is important in measuring front office function because it has little to do with clean claim submission or effective follow-up.

Percentage of Accounts Receivable Beyond X Days (PARBX)

PARBX resolves the sensitivity issue of the DAR metric. It offers a simple billing process metric that's not dependent on the charge. Its graphic representation has a skewed bell shape (Figures 12 and 13).

Its steepness represents billing process quality; a steep curve and thin tail means a healthy billing process, while a flat bell and fat tail means billing problems. According to the MGMA survey, 25%–35% of the average family practice's accounts receivables were more than 120 days old in 1997. This number has improved down to 17.7% in 2004.[59]

---

[59] Lowes, "Practice Pointers."

Figure 12. Bad Billing Performance

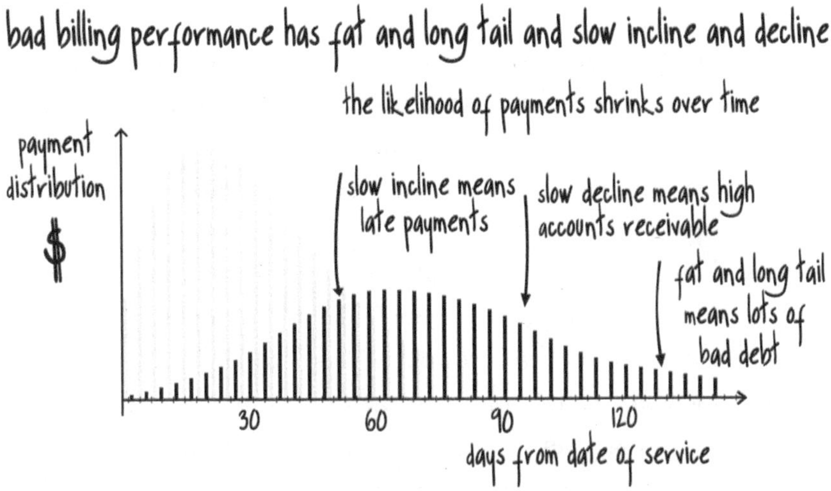

The likelihood of payment shrinks with each passing day.

Figure 13. Good Billing Performance

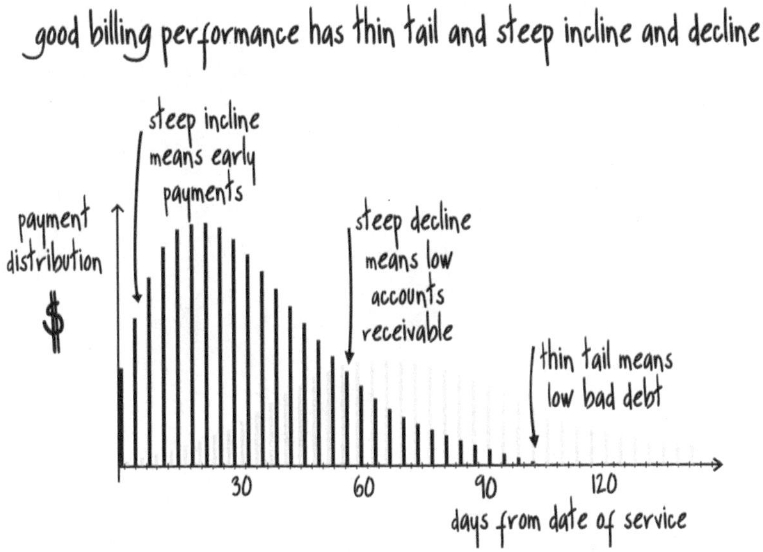

The sooner the payments are received,
the more likely it is that every claim will be paid in full.

Summary

In summary, comprehensive metrics that are not dependent on charges, such as PARBX, are more informative and objective than collection ratios. However, these metrics alone fall short of identifying specific areas for billing process improvement. Modern technology helps to identify billing bottlenecks because it allows the interactive review of multiple metrics along different aggregation dimensions. For instance, the PARBX metric is especially helpful to identify patterns of problem claims containing specific payers or CPT codes. Further, modern Vericle-like technologies enable the comparison of every payment with the allowed amount and subsequent appeal on every denial, effectively reducing the average percentage of accounts receivable to low single digits.

Chapter 17

What Can Clean Claims Tell Us About Payer-Provider Conflict?

Dr. Noah Payne shook his head in disbelief: the practice reimbursements shrank, instead of climbed, in response to the recent hiring of Dr. Inna Ternist.[60] The new doctor clearly added to the total number of patients seen, yet overall payments did not reflect the added charges. Perhaps the new claims weren't created, submitted, or paid? Dr. Noah remembered noticing the growing pile of rejected and denied claims accumulating dust on his desk—he never had the time to review them. How many of these claims were clean? How many required manual review and correction?

Dr. Noah looked at his Vericle screen and began analyzing the numbers. The system showed 58% clean claims (percentage clean claims, or PCC). In other words, almost half of the claims required manual correction. Who could be causing such a high level of problems—the practice, the billing service, or the payer? Dr. Noah instinctively felt that the billing service was negligent about the data entry process and kept introducing massive data errors. But the service man-

[60] This is a real-life example. However, most names have been changed.

ager was quick to explain their rigorous quality assurance process for data entry. What else could cause such a high level of manual work in a seemingly streamlined process?

Trying to discover a pattern, Dr. Noah looked for a root cause dimension. He drilled into 99213—the most frequent CPT code for his practice. Vericle showed 3,135 claims for the 99213 code, and these had an above-average 62 PCC (62% clean claims).

Having isolated the most frequent CPT code, Dr. Noah thought about other dimensions that influence PCC. He hypothesized that if all doctors in his practice had the same coding skills, and assuming uniform distribution of errors, there should be no PCC variance across the doctors. Yet, a quick click on a Vericle screen confirmed his suspicion that different doctors maintained slightly different coding skills.

	Dr. Ted	Dr. Lori	Dr. Inna	Dr. Noah
Claims	1,554	865	194	516
PCC for a Single CPT (99213)	63%	62%	61%	60%

Next, Dr. Noah switched his attention to PCC distribution across the financial classes. Again, he hypothesized that if all payers used the same rules to deny claims, then there should be no difference in the average PCC for different payers, subject to a uniform distribution of errors over a large sample of submitted and paid claims. Yet the numbers showed a significant (30%) variation of PCC for the same CPT code:

82	UnitedHealthcare
73	Horizon Blue Cross Blue Shield of New Jersey
64	Oxford
59	Aetna
59	Medicare

51 CIGNA

This confirmed his conclusion that different payers used different rules to deny and underpay claims (Figure 14).

Figure 14. "Clean Claim" Distribution by Payers

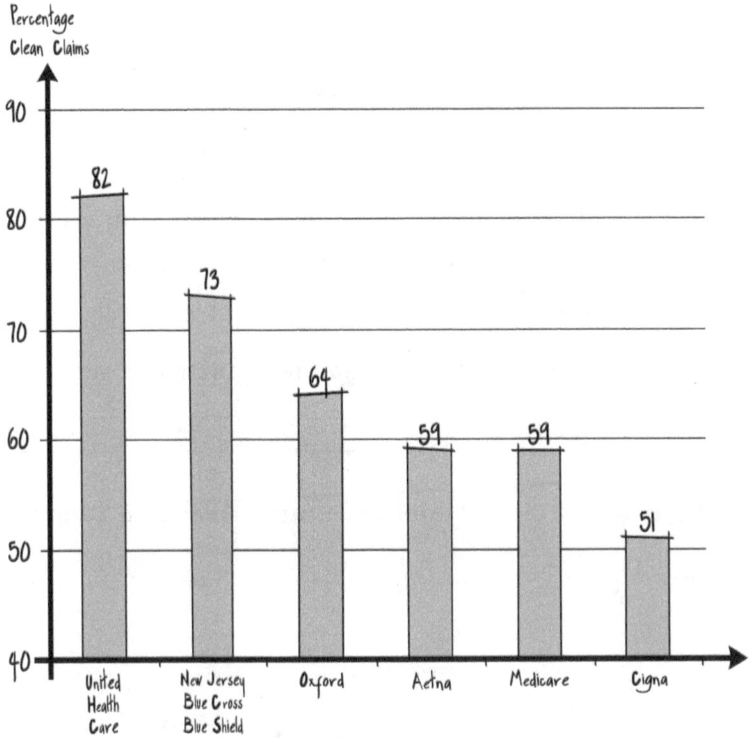

Dr. Noah recalled an article about PacifiCare, a California insurance company, being fined after an audit revealed that 30% of their HMO claims were wrongly denied and 29% of their disputes with doctors were handled incorrectly (see Chapter 2).[61] Dr. Noah's findings roughly matched the PacifiCare audit—the insurance companies were

[61] Chan, "PacifiCare Fined."

failing anywhere between 18% and 49% of his claims, and each insurance company showed a different failure rate, depending on their system for failing submitted claims.

Finally, Dr. Noah's thought about his billing service operation. Did his billing service systematically work to discover failed claims and improve its response to such discoveries? Was there a pattern in the PCC, perhaps an occasional drop that might reflect a response to various payers' initiatives? Conversely, was there any evidence of a systematic improvement effort? To answer his question, he needed a chart of the distribution of a single CPT code's clean claim percentage over the entire year. In his mind, PCC should level out between occasional drops and climbs, hopefully settling at a slightly higher level after each time. He was looking for an overall improvement through the year. Indeed, Vericle confirmed his expectations (Table 4 and Figure 15).

Table 4. Percentage Clean Claim Distribution

	Jan	Feb	Mar	Apr	May	Jun	Jul	Aug	Sep	Oct	Nov	Dec
PCC	46	39	52	55	63	67	72	69	72	68	74	73

Figure 15. "Clean Claim" Evolution Over One Year

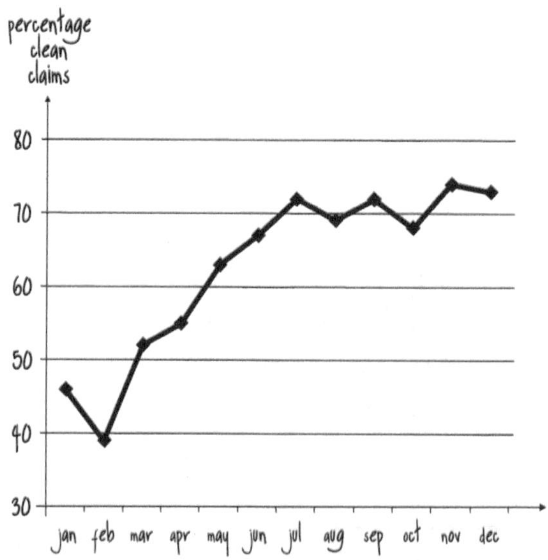

In summary, Dr. Noah concluded that PCC must be a time-dependent function, which drops and climbs depending on four important factors. Specifically, PCC goes down in response to (a) continuous *payer* initiatives to impede billing—rejecting, losing, delaying, and underpaying claims; (b) the *practice* missing or incorrectly submitting demographics and coding information; or (c) the *billing service* entering erroneous or inconsistent data. PCC improves in response to a concerted effort by both the practice and the billing service to discover, correct, and avoid demographic, coding, and data entry problems. Large-scale medical billing networks create the necessary volumes and resulting economies of scale that enable the payment analyses to discover systemic claims processing problems.

Chapter 18

Billing Transparency

Arcane terminology and complex rules for payer- and time-dependent claim validity and pricing interpretation plague the medical billing industry. This results in massive payments of invalid or ineligible claims and in denials of error-free claims. The amount and complexity of billing information make it very difficult for the doctor to maintain compliance and to identify and resolve errors and underpayments.

"With integrated billing transparency, I see for myself how Vericle leverages every opportunity to expedite payments of healthcare insurance claims in a continuous 24/7 effort. It has enabled 27% revenue gain over [the] past billing process," says Doug Cassel, MD, director of Interventional Radiology at Hoag Memorial Hospital in Newport Beach, California.

Greater visibility of internal process activities promotes teamwork, increases client satisfaction, and assists in process streamlining. Billing service transparency allows participants of the billing process to expedite error identification and resolution, resulting in reduced overpayments and underpayments as well as improved regulatory compliance.

Billing Dashboard as Main Transparency Mechanism

Selecting meaningful and intuitive indicators for the billing process performance is a mission-critical stage in creating a useful transparency mechanism. A "dashboard" that presents the most meaningful data must be easy to find and simple to interpret. The cumulative experience of hundreds of doctors using Vericle has shown that a dashboard containing nine specific indicators expedites the development of intuitive and powerful transparency mechanisms:

1. Month-to-date collections
2. Total failed or denied claims
3. Aggregate failed or denied claims in the follow-up queue
4. Dollar amount of accounts receivable (A/R) below 30 days
5. Dollar amount of A/R from 31–120 days
6. Dollar amount of A/R greater than 120 days
7. Percentage of A/R below 30 days
8. Percentage of A/R from 31–120 days
9. Percentage of A/R greater than 120 days

Note that the national average of accounts receivable above 120 days hovers around 18%.[62] Therefore, a well-performing outsourced billing service must deliver an A/R above 120 days that's significantly below 18%. Specifically, to justify its fees, an outsourced billing service must measure its A/R above 120 days at somewhere around 5%.

Drill-down Functionality, Reporting, and Transparency

An advanced dashboard allows a drill-down for more detail by pointing and clicking directly on the screen. At the minimum, the fol-

---

[62] Lowes, "Practice Pointers."

lowing features must be available (see more detail in Chapter 10:

- **Operational report** – Shows total claims and dollar amounts submitted, paid, adjusted, written off, and failed. It allows a breakdown by CPT code, payer, referral, or any combination.
- **Denials report** – Shows the list of denied claims and a log of follow-up actions. When sorting it by the amount paid, you can determine the smallest payment that the billing service will fight for.
- **Compliance report** – Shows the potential for post-payment audit, and itemizes compliance violations.

These reports allow multiple dimensions for data presentation by single parameter—such as payer, CPT code, provider, or referring physician—or by more complex parameter combinations—such as pairs of payer-CPT code, provider-CPT code, or referring physician-CPT code.

Complexity Considerations

Note that even a small single-provider practice working with 20 CPT codes and 20 payers has 400 (20 x 20) payer-CPT code pairs. Therefore, an online report comparing month-to-date collections between current and previous years requires a powerful database query capability. Moreover, automation of such queries—like "find the worst-performing payer for the best-performing CPT code"—requires OLAP (online analytical processing) technology.

Summary

Billing transparency is a necessary feature of a modern and accountable billing service. It allows the practice owner to know both the big picture and the minute detail of the billing process. To observe every step of the billing process on a continuous 24/7 basis, reporting must be available using a secure, HIPAA-compliant connection over the Internet. While traditional services have delivered monthly paper reports, modern technology allows the delivery of continuously updated and meaningful billing performance data.

Chapter 19

Claim Denial Management

Partial denials cause the average medical practice to lose as much as 11% of its revenue.[63] Denial management is difficult because of the complexity of denial causes, payer variety, and claim volume. Systematic denial management requires measurement, early claim validation, comprehensive monitoring, and customized tracking of the appeals process.

In a high-volume clinic, the only practical way to manage denials is to use computer technology and follow a four-step procedure:

1. **Prevent mistakes during claim submission** – This can be accomplished with a built-in claim validation procedure that includes payer-specific tests. Such tests ("pre-submission scrubbing") compare every claim with Correct Coding Initiative (CCI) regulations; diligently review modifiers used to differentiate between procedures on the same claim; and compare the charged amount with the allowed amount, according to previous experience or the previous

[63] Capko, "Physicians Practice Pearls."

contract, to avoid undercharging.

2. **Identify underpayments** – This involves comparing the payment with the allowed amount, identifying zero-paid items, and evaluating payment timeliness. The results of this stage should be displayed in a comprehensive underpayment report sorted by payer, provider, claim identification, and the amount of underpayment.

3. **Appeal denials** – Appeal management includes appeal prioritization, preparation of arguments and documentation, tracking, and escalation. Note that CCI spells out bundling standards, but the number of standard interpretations grows in step with the number of payers. Therefore, CCI provides the justification basis for an appeal, and every appeal must be argued on its own merits, including medical notes. The denial appeal process is typically managed with a custom process tracking system, such as TrackLogix.

4. **Measure denial rates** – You cannot manage what you don't measure. By measuring denial rates and observing payment trends, you can see if your process requires modifications.

As mentioned in Chapter 3, denial risk is not uniform across all claims. Certain classes of claims run significantly higher denial risks, depending on three factors:

1. **Claim complexity**
    a. Modifiers
    b. Multiple line items

2. **Temporary constraints**
    a. Patient constraint (e.g., claim submission during global periods)
    b. Payer constraint (e.g., claim submission timing proximity to start of fiscal year)
    c. Procedure constraint (e.g., experimental services)

3. **Payer idiosyncrasies**
    a. Bundled services
    b. Disputed medical necessity

For complex claims, most payers pay the full amount for one line item, but then pay only a percentage of the remaining items. This payment approach creates two opportunities for underpayment:

1. The order of paid items
2. The payment percentage of remaining items

Next, temporary constraints often cause payment errors because of the misapplication of constraints. For instance, claims submitted during the global period for services unrelated to the global period are often denied. Similar mistakes may occur at the start of the fiscal year due to misapplying rules for deductibles or outdated fee schedules.

Finally, payers often vary in their interpretations of Correct Coding Initiative (CCI) bundling rules or coverage of certain services. Developing sensitivity to such idiosyncrasies is a key to full and timely payments.

Summary

Powerful Vericle-like technology helps you manage denial appeals nationwide and stay current until problem resolution is complete.

Every time one billing problem is solved, the newly gained knowledge is encoded for recycling. Sharing billing expertise in a centralized billing knowledge base expedites future problem resolution.

Chapter 20

To Par or Not to Par: A Medical Billing Dilemma in Anticipation of Proposed Medicare Cuts

As each year end approaches, providers face the participation-nonparticipation dilemma—status change notifications are accepted until January 1 only. For example, starting in 2007, doctors had to choose between higher reimbursements and patient collections or lower reimbursement and direct deposit. The choice was complicated because Congress had not yet completed debating an upcoming 10.1% Medicare cut to physicians. Congress's delay and the unprecedented proposed cut size dramatized the possibility of locking in doctors for another year under a newly reduced fee schedule, thereby raising the urgency and importance of this decision.

American Medical Association (AMA) president Ron Davis, MD, commented on this proposed cut: "Unless Congress takes immediate action . . . Medicare will begin across-the-board cuts on January 1 [2008]. Congressional action is not guaranteed, so physicians interested in changing their Medicare participation status for 2008 should review the information now, fill out the forms and prepare to mail them prior to December 31."[64] Although Congress eventually cancelled the 10% cut for now, the same question will surface again the next year.

Physicians have three options for Medicare—participation (PAR), nonparticipation (non-PAR), and private contracting:

1. **Participation** – Physicians participating in Medicare (PAR) agree to standard Medicare fees for every submitted claim. The participating doctor gives up the right to "balance-bill" patients for the difference between the standard Medicare fee and doctor's "reasonable and customary" fee. But the predictability of payment timing and the convenience of direct deposit using electronic fund transfer (EFT) are major participation decision factors: first, Medicare typically pays electronically submitted "clean" claims within 14 days of claim submission, and second, Medicare pays the physician directly.
2. **Nonparticipation** – Nonparticipating physicians (non-PAR) can decide on a per-patient basis to accept the reduced fee (accept "assignment") or balance-bill patients up to 15% more. Therefore, a non-PAR physician who balance-bills every patient may receive up to 9.25% more than a PAR doctor for the same services. The downside of non-PAR is that Medicare reimburses patients directly, and physicians must invoice patients for the full amount: the payment, co-payment, and balance-billing charge. If physicians postpone invoicing patients until the patients receive their insurance reimbursements, then the doctors risks collection problems with financially irresponsible patients.
3. **Private contracting** – Private contracting means that physicians opt out of Medicare completely for at least two

[64] Glendinning, "Looming Medicare Pay Cut."

years. During these two years, neither the opted-out physicians nor their patients can bill Medicare for any services.

Other PAR versus non-PAR decision considerations are as follows:

1. **Collections work-around** – The number of collection problems from patients may be negligent, or problems can be completely eliminated if physicians collect the entire fee at the time of visit.
2. **Saving grace** – Financing out-of-pocket fees for more needy patients, while collecting higher fees from balance-billed patients, might be the "saving grace" alternative to turning away patients.
3. **Patient perception** – Patients who are used to having all of their medical costs covered by a system of primary, secondary—and, perhaps, tertiary—insurance companies might protest higher out-of-pocket fees.

Note also that the "participation dilemma" is not exclusive to Medicare. Some insurance companies—e.g., Oxford (UnitedHealthcare) and CIGNA—still send checks to non-PAR doctors. However, others—like Horizon Blue Cross Blue Shield of New Jersey—penalize non-PAR doctors by paying directly to patients.

The AMA outlines participation options and status change procedures: "When considering whether to be non-PAR, however, physicians should consider whether their total revenues from Medicare, including amounts the program pays, patient co-pays and balance billing, would exceed their total revenues as PAR physicians, particularly in light of collection costs, bad debts and claims for which they do accept assignment."[65]

---

[65] American Medical Association, *Medicare Participation Options*.

Chapter 21

Lost Revenue Discovery with OLAP

The average medical practice may lose as much as 11% of its revenue due to underpayments. To avoid unrecoverable losses, some providers discontinue servicing patients insured by the worst-performing payers. Unfortunately, such a drastic loss-reduction measure may boomerang and increase losses, depending on the complexity of referral relationships. This chapter outlines limitations of traditional database queries that are used to identify payer candidates for contract termination, and it demonstrates alternative decision choices with superior performance, in terms of revenue and risk management, facilitated with online analytical processing (OLAP) technology.

First-Order SQL Queries for A/R Analysis

Traditional accounts receivable analysis includes identifying payers that systematically underpay and refuse denial appeals. Such analysis is based on simple queries that are designed to identify the best CPT code or the worst payer in absolute terms:

- Comparison of revenue for various CPT codes for a given

time period

- Comparison of underpayments for various payers for a given time period
- Comparison of denials for various payers for a given time period

Single-key database indexing is a standard measure to improve the time performance of such queries. It builds an ordered relationship within the data elements, based on the value of the selected metric. But single-key indexing precludes the implementation of more complex queries, like "Who is the payer that underpays the most for the best CPT code?" or "Who is the worst referring physician for my worst payer?" And single-key indexing requires complex SQL programming skills because of the need to store and process intermediate results. Therefore, ranking the data elements along a single attribute forces a limited choice for management decision:

- Ignore the problem
- Renegotiate the contract with the payer
- Stop serving patients insured by the worst payer

But to find more subtle solutions, the office manager requires the ability to aggregate and drill into data and formulate queries in real time, in response to observed results to the previous queries. Specifically, a low-frequency, underperforming payer with a high degree of underpayment may not be as detrimental to the office as a high-frequency, underperforming payer with a low degree of underpayment. Contract termination with a wrong payer may accomplish the opposite result for practice goals in terms of revenue maximization and workload reduction. Additionally, a decision to stop serving patients insured by any one payer may reduce the referral volume of other patients across all payers for a particular referring physician.

Combinatorial (Second-Order SQL) Queries

Fortunately, modern database query technology can address both limitations by enabling "second-order SQL" queries, which allow data manipulation based on multiple criteria and using combinations of such criteria.

In our case, second-degree SQL queries allow finding the worst payer for the best-revenue-generating code. Such a discriminating approach allows focusing on higher-priority items first, resulting in more effective management. In general, the manager performs a custom comparison of payers according to the following four-step sequence:

1. Select metrics (e.g., percent paid, percent accounts receivable beyond 120 days, percent denials)
2. Select dimensions (providers, payers, CPT codes, ICD-9 codes, referring physicians)
3. Partition
4. Aggregate, drill down, pivot

Worst Payer Query

To find a payer with the highest amount of underpayments for the most frequent CPT code, a second-order SQL query can be written along the following lines:

> For a given time-interval,
> Select payers
> Where the sum of underpayments over
> (all CPT codes where Revenue > Revenue Threshold)
> > Underpayment Threshold

Worst Referring Physician Query

To avoid the risk of losing referrals from better-performing payers, the manager may consider severing the referral relationship with some referring physicians instead of payers. In such a case, the distribution of patients across various payers plays an important role for each referring physician. A single combinatorial query may fetch the worst referring physician as follows:

> For a given time-interval,
> Select referring physicians
> Where Revenue for the Worst Payer > Threshold

Summary

Underpayment management involves all phases of claims processing, and it requires powerful Vericle-like computing platforms for exhaustive comparisons of payments versus allowed amounts and subsequent appeal management. OLAP (online analytical processing) allows better analysis of accounts receivable and more effective management because of the ability to handle queries with functions of multiple attributes and dimensions. Note that in the absence of a native OLAP mechanism, effective Vericle-like billing platforms allow similarly powerful analysis by introducing intermediary steps. Such steps may add insight to analysis and improve decision quality.

Part IV

Compliance and Audit

It was much pleasanter at home, when one wasn't always growing larger and smaller, and being ordered about by mice and rabbits.

—Alice
Alice's Adventures in Wonderland
Lewis Carroll

Compliance and audit risk services improve with each additional practice using Vericle. Vericle leverages the network effect to improve these services in several ways, which are discussed in Part IV. It presents four chapters, one focused on HIPAA compliance and rest on medical note management compliance, provider audit risks, and the False Claims Act (FCA).

Both HIPAA and medical note management compliance are crucially important for practice management, and both must be handled effectively and unobtrusively, without impeding practice productivity. HIPAA compliance emphasizes security and privacy, while medical note management compliance emphasizes medical necessity.

Accordingly, HIPAA compliance employs mostly technical tools and procedures to lock information away and to ensure secure access on a "need to know" basis, while medical note compliance procedures use technology and processes to track medical progress and monitor potential payment rule violation likelihood and audit exposure. At the end, successfully implementing both HIPAA and medical note compliance depends on discipline and adequate technology.

Erum Raza is a corporate attorney and associate in the Princeton, New Jersey, office of Fox Rothschild LLP. Ms. Raza specializes in healthcare law and business transactions, and she has contributed two chapters that focus on FCA risk management.

Chapter 22

HIPAA Compliance and Role-Based Access Control

HIPAA compliance requires special focus and effort, as failure to comply carries significant risk of damage and penalties. A practice with multiple separate systems for patient scheduling, electronic medical records, and billing requires multiple and separate HIPAA management efforts. This chapter presents an integrated approach to HIPAA compliance and outlines key HIPAA terminology, principles, and requirements to help the practice owner ensure compliance by medical billing services and software vendors.

The last decade of the previous century witnessed accelerating proliferation of digital technology in healthcare, which, along with reduced costs and greater service quality, introduced new and greater risks for accidental disclosure of personal health information.

The Health Insurance Portability and Accountability Act (HIPAA) was passed by Congress in 1996 to establish national standards for privacy and security of personal health data. The Privacy Rule, a component of HIPAA written by the U.S. Department of Health and Human Services, took effect on April 14, 2003.

Failure to comply with HIPAA risks accreditation and reputation damage, lawsuits by the federal government, financial penalties (ranging from $100 to $250,000), and imprisonment (ranging from 1 year to 10 years).

Protected Health Information (PHI)

The key term of HIPAA is protected health information (PHI), which includes anything that can be used to identify an individual and any information shared with other healthcare providers or clearinghouses in any media (digital, verbal, recorded voice, faxed, printed, or written).

Information that can be used to identify an individual includes the following:

1. Name
2. Dates (except year)
3. ZIP code of more than 3 digits, telephone and fax numbers, email address
4. Social Security numbers
5. Medical record numbers
6. Health plan numbers
7. License numbers
8. Photographs

Information shared with other healthcare providers or clearinghouses include the following:

1. Nursing and physician notes
2. Billing and other treatment records

Principles of HIPAA

HIPAA intends to allow the smooth flow of PHI for healthcare operations subject to a patient's consent, but it prohibits any flow of unauthorized PHI for any other purposes. Healthcare operations include treatment, payment, care quality assessment, competence review training, accreditation, insurance rating, auditing, and legal procedures.

HIPAA promotes fair information practices and requires those with access to PHI to safeguard it. Fair information practices means that a patient must be allowed the following:

1. Access to PHI
2. Corrections for errors and completeness
3. Knowledge of others who use PHI

Safeguarding of PHI means that anybody who holds PHI must meet these requirements:

1. Be accountable for its use and disclosure
2. Have a legal recourse to combat violations

HIPAA Implementation Process

HIPAA implementation begins upon making assumptions about the PHI disclosure threat model. The implementation includes both preemptive and retroactive controls, and it involves process, technology, and personnel aspects.

A threat model helps us understand the purpose of the HIPAA implementation process. It includes assumptions about the following:

1. Threat nature (e.g., accidental disclosure by insiders, access for profit)

2. Source of threat (e.g., outsider or insider)
3. Means of potential threat (e.g., break-in, physical intrusion, computer hack, virus)
4. Specific kind of data at risk (e.g., patient identification, financials, or medical records)
5. Scale (e.g., how many patient records are threatened)

The HIPAA process must include a clearly stated policy, educational materials and events, a clear enforcement means, a schedule for testing of HIPAA compliance, and a means for the continued transparency about HIPAA compliance. A stated policy typically includes a statement of least privilege (the least amount of privileged data necessary to complete the job), the definition of PHI, and incident monitoring and reporting procedures. Educational materials may include case studies, control questions, and a schedule of review seminars for personnel.

Technology Requirements for HIPAA Compliance

Technology implementation of HIPAA proceeds in stages, from logical data definition to the physical data center to the network.

1. **To assure physical data center security**, the manager must do the following:
    a. Lock the data center
    b. Manage the access list
    c. Track data center access with closed-circuit TV cameras to monitor both internal and external building activities
    d. Protect access to the data center with 24/7 on-site security
    e. Protect backup data

f. Test the recovery procedure

2. **For network security**, the data center must have special facilities for the following:
   a. Secure networking – firewall protection, encrypted data transfer only
   b. Network access monitoring and report auditing

3. **For data security**, the manager must have the following:
   a. Individual authentication – individual logins and passwords
   b. Role-based access control (see the next section)
   c. Audit trails – all access to all data fields tracked and recorded
   d. Data discipline – limited ability to download data

Role-Based Access Control (RBAC)

RBAC improves the convenience and flexibility of systems management. Greater convenience helps reduce the errors of commission and omission in granting access privileges to users. Greater flexibility helps implement the policy of least privilege, where users are granted only as many privileges as needed to complete their jobs.

RBAC promotes economies of scale, because the frequency of role definition changes for a single user is higher than the frequency of role definition changes across an entire organization. Thus, to make a massive change of privileges for a large number of users with the same set of privileges, the administrator makes changes only to the role definition.

Hierarchical RBAC also promotes economies of scale and reduces the likelihood of errors. It allows redefining roles by inheriting privileges assigned to roles in the higher hierarchical level.

RBAC is based on establishing a set of user profiles or roles according to responsibilities. Each role has a predefined set of privileges. The user acquires privileges by receiving membership in the role or assignment of a profile by the administrator.

Every time the definition of the role changes, along with the set of privileges that's required to complete the job associated with the role, the administrator needs only to redefine the role's privileges. The privileges of all users who have this role are automatically redefined.

Similarly, if the role of a single user is changed, the only operation that needs to be performed is reassigning the user profile, which automatically redefines the user's access privileges according to the new profile.

Summary

HIPAA compliance requires special practice management attention. A practice with multiple and separate systems for scheduling, electronic medical records, and billing requires multiple and separate HIPAA management efforts. An integrated system reduces the complexity of HIPAA implementation. By outsourcing technology to a HIPAA-compliant vendor of a Vericle-like technology solution on an ASP or SaaS basis, HIPAA management overhead can be eliminated.

Chapter 23

Pre-Payment and Post-Payment Audits

Mistaken payments add up to an estimated $200 billion annually, exceeding 10% of national healthcare costs.[66] Other party liability (OPL) alone—i.e., claims that should be paid by somebody else—comprise $68 billion annually, or 3.6% of national healthcare costs. The enormity of potential savings due to improved claims processing continues to attract the attention and focus of resources. Insurance profitability experts believe that a payment scrutiny program can be as successful a profit-building strategy for insurance companies as raising premiums or adding members. A growing industry of outsourced technology and services to avoid mistaken payments is also symptomatic of the growing demand for such services. Some vendors cite cumulative payment savings as high as $3 billion.[67]

However, avoiding mistaken payments is difficult because of four constraints: the volume of claims, the disparate and disconnected sources of relevant information, the resource-intensive manual processes needed to identify and investigate recovery opportunities, and

[66] Overfield, *The Cost of Health Care Overpayments.*

[67] Ibid.

regulatory requirements for timely payments.

To manage these difficulties, many payers have adopted a two-phase "pay and refund" approach to minimize payment. The second phase of this approach is designed to correct any mistakes made during the first phase. Each of the phases can be further divided into two subphases. Specifically, the initial phase splits into pre-payment review and timely payment of valid items, while the final phase includes post-payment audits and refunds of items proven invalid during the audit.

Pre-Payment Review

Pre-payment review typically proceeds in two stages: identification and confirmation. Potential overpayment identification requires cross-referencing multiple systems that manage provider enrollment, authorizations, recovery case management, and call centers for both insured and providers.

Overpayment confirmation uses Correct Coding Initiative (CCI), local medical review policies (LMRPs), and other rules to categorize the potential overpayments into contractual/clinical, eligibility, coordination of benefits, or duplicate payments. Overpayment confirmation typically includes tests for inter-claim, intra-claim, or cross-claim inconsistencies; lifetime duplicates; date range duplicates; re-bundling; inappropriate modifier codes; wrong E&M crosswalk; upcoded or undercoded visit level; etc.

Pre-payment review requires powerful database technology. Most of the pre-payment claim review process can be automated along with the subsequent denial notice or explanation of benefits (EOB).

Post-Payment Audit

In contrast, post-payment audits tend to consume more resources during each of the audit stages:

1. **Target identification** – An audit identification report shows total annual revenue and the degree of variance between the audit target and peers in the same specialty and geography. The product of the two numbers is proportional to the expected gain from the audit, essentially providing a natural audit ranking (Figure 16).

Figure 16. Statistical Audit Flagging

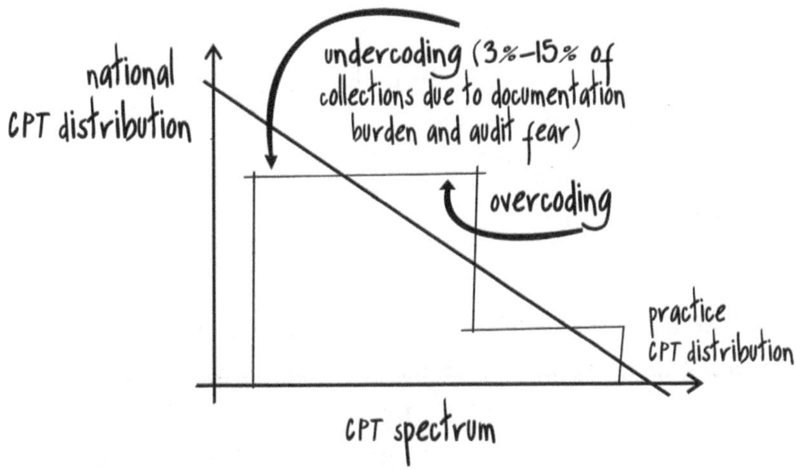

Superposition of billing distributions reveals patterns of nonconformity.

2. **Audit preparation** – A higher return to the payer is the key advantage of a carefully designed and executed post-payment audit. Audit preparation starts with a review of the audit target selection, which is the result of provider profiling and variance reporting. This stage includes a list of claims paid in the past that are most likely to fall outside of a standard distribution of the peer group.

3. **Audit execution** – The auditor requests and analyzes

medical notes supporting the data reflected in the sample of paid claims that are produced at the audit preparation stage. The auditor's objective is to establish the proportion of claims found unsupported by reviewed medical notes within the set of the audited sample (percent of overpayment).

4. **Refund (and penalty) extrapolation** – The auditor extrapolates the refund as the product of the percent of overpayment and the total payments by the auditing insurance carrier for the past six years.

5. **Negotiation**

6. **Settlement**

Some stages—such as audit execution, negotiation, and settlement—must be entirely manual and may require highly skilled and experienced personnel. Other stages—such as verification of overpayment amount and currency, identification of overpayment reason, and audit prioritization—may be partially automated, using rule-based technology to identify procedure repetition, high payments per day, surge analysis, unusual modifiers, unusual procedure rates, geographic improbabilities, or 5/50 patterns.[68] External resources might be added at this stage to consult provider watch lists, Office of Inspector General (OIG) sanctions databases, or high-risk address databases.

Summary

A full-scale implementation of payment scrutiny requires sophisti-

[68] A 5/50 pattern is when five CPT codes make up more than 50% of total CPT code frequencies in a given sample.

cated processes to handle pre-payment claim reviews and post-payment audits, and such processes use advanced fraud detection technology. Pre-payment claim reviews are less expensive than post-payment audits and therefore can be applied to every claim, while post-payment audits must be carefully targeted. A system to manage the overpayment recovery process must include claim identification, claim history, provider and insured information, medical notes, insured services call center notes, authorizations, etc. Without the ability to efficiently manage a large volume of recovery cases, the risk for errors or missed payment deadlines is high, resulting in missed recovery opportunities.

Chapter 24

Exposure to Liability under the Federal False Claims Act

Invited Chapter
Erum Raza, Esq.

In 2008, the best and perhaps most common way for the federal government to "cut government spending" and "maintain the viability of the healthcare industry" has been to combat healthcare fraud and abuse through actively enforcing federal antifraud compliance laws against physicians and other healthcare providers. This chapter discusses how the federal False Claims Act (FCA, or the Act)[69] can be enforced against physicians for improper coding and billing practices as well as how investigations comes about. The next chapter covers tips on how physicians can avoid investigation of their medical practice and/or liability under the FCA.

---

[69] False Claims Act, 31 U.S.C. § 3729, et seq.

Exposure to Liability under the FCA

Under the FCA, any physician, hospital, or other healthcare provider[70] that participates in a federally funded healthcare program—such as Medicare, Medicaid, or TRICARE[71]—can be subject to significant civil monetary penalties and criminal liability for submitting improperly coded claims for payment to a federally funded healthcare program and/or engaging in any of the following practices, among many others, in violation of the FCA:

- Upcoding (e.g., billing for complex services when only simple services were performed)
- Phantom billing (e.g., billing for tests not performed)
- Performing medically "inappropriate" or "unnecessary" procedures
- Charging for equipment and/or supplies that were not ordered or used
- Billing for new and expensive equipment, but providing patients with used and inexpensive equipment
- Reflex testing (e.g., automatically running a test whenever the results of another test fall within a certain range)
- Unbundling (e.g., using two or more CPT codes, instead of one inclusive code for a defined panel, when rules and regulations require bundling of such claims)
- Submitting multiple bills in order to obtain higher reimbursement for tests and services performed within a specified time period, and which should have been submitted as a single bill

[70] This chapter primarily focuses on *physician* liability under the FCA, as opposed to *hospital* liability.

[71] TRICARE is the health care plan for military personnel, military retirees, and their dependents.

- Double billing, or charging more than once for the same services (e.g., billing once using an individual code, and again as part of a bundled set of tests)
- Routinely waiving patient co-payments

If physicians are found to have violated the FCA for *any* reason, *whether intentionally or not*, they may be required to pay the federal government "treble damages," or up to three times the amount of any federal monies that were lost as a result of improper reimbursement. Additionally, the FCA has an additional penalty for violations—$5,500 to $11,000 *per claim*—if the physician knowingly submitted or caused the submission of a false or fraudulent claim to the United States.[72] More often than not, physicians who have FCA claims brought against them will settle the claims at a high cost; this is in lieu of potentially lengthy, burdensome, and professionally and personally disparaging litigation. Typically, investigations are initiated because a "whistleblower" reports suspicious activity to the authorities or because the medical practice is audited by an independent auditor. This topic is discussed in greater detail later in this chapter.

Enacted in 1863 at the height of the Civil War, the FCA was originally created to combat deceptive practices of private contractors doing business with the federal government; these contractors defrauded the government by supplying Union Army troops with defective products and faulty equipment. Over the past hundred years, the FCA has been applied much more broadly, and today it's primarily used to prevent fraud and abuse in the healthcare industry. Certain states, such as New Jersey, have enacted their own versions of the FCA that can subject physicians to additional liability.[73]

---

[72] False Claims Act, 31 U.S.C. 3729 (a).

[73] In addition to the FCA, on February 8, 2006, Congress enacted the Deficit Reduction Act of 2005 (DRA), Pub. L. No. 109-171, § 6031, to further combat healthcare fraud and abuse. Section 6031 of the DRA encourages states to enact their own false claims acts to establish state liability for submitting false or

You Can Be Liable Even if You Didn't Have the Intent to Defraud

False claims cases/investigations often are based on the theory that the physician billed for services that were not reimbursable by Medicare because they were (a) noncovered screenings; (b) not reasonable and necessary; and (c) based on false, inappropriate, and/or inadequate diagnosis. Notably, under the FCA, physicians may be held responsible even if they were *unaware* that specific false claims were filed on their behalf; this is because the FCA imposes a responsibility on providers to supervise the billing function to make sure it's carried out in accordance with the law.[74] Moreover, if providers find out that they received payments for charges that were improperly submitted, they can be held criminally liable as well as be required to pay civil monetary damages if they *don't report a known error.*[75] While voluntary disclosure of known errors will not absolve physicians of their responsibility under the FCA, it will likely encourage prosecutors to settle for penalties less than treble damages.

---

fraudulent claims for payment to state-funded programs. The DRA also gives states financial incentives to enact such antifraud legislation. In January 2008, the New Jersey Assembly unanimously passed a state version of the FCA, which was signed into law by Governor Corzine on January 14, 2008. The New Jersey false claims act is based on the federal FCA; it imposes similar penalties on violators and provides financial incentives to whistleblowers. Twenty-two other states have enacted versions of the FCA: Arkansas, California, Delaware, Florida, Georgia, Hawaii, Illinois, Indiana, Louisiana, Massachusetts, Michigan, Missouri, Montana, Nevada, New Hampshire, New Mexico, New York, Oklahoma, Rhode Island, Tennessee, Texas, Virginia, and the District of Columbia.

[74] The FCA provides that people may be liable for a violation if they (1) had "actual knowledge of the falsely submitted information; (2) acted in deliberate ignorance of the truth or falsity of the information; or (3) acted in reckless disregard of the truth or falsity of the information." The FCA also clearly states that "no proof of specific intent to defraud is required" to prove a violation of the FCA (31 U.S.C. 3729[b]).

[75] Health Insurance Portability and Accountability Act (HIPAA), 42 U.S.C. 1320-7b(a)(3).

Spotlight on Real-life Examples

The Public Affairs branch of the United States Department of Justice (DOJ) and local state U.S. Attorneys' Offices publicly disclose many details about investigations and cases alleging healthcare fraud and FCA violations. A significant amount of information can be accessed from the DOJ's website (www.usdoj.gov)—including copies of filed complaints, settlement agreements reached between the government and defendants, and briefs filed on behalf of the government. The following are some summaries of recent investigations, settlements, and decisions of note obtained from the DOJ website:

2007 – Dr. Marquez (Texas)

The United States and State of Texas settled an FCA lawsuit against a physician, Dr. Marquez, and two hospitals with which he was affiliated and had an ownership interest. The investigation began in 2002 when another physician working with Dr. Marquez approached federal authorities in a qui tam ("whistleblower") lawsuit in which he alleged that Dr. Marquez was defrauding Medicare and Medicaid by billing for services not rendered as represented.[76]

The federal government joined in the lawsuit and filed its own complaint in September 2006. The government's complaint alleged that Dr. Marquez, individually and through defendant hospitals, "made false claims and false statements to the United States in connection with claims for reimbursement he submitted for his treatment of Medicare and Medicaid patients." It alleged that Dr. Marquez billed for services that were not rendered, not rendered as represented, and/or

[76] "Qui tam" is Latin phrase meaning "he who brings a case on behalf of our lord the King, as well as for himself." In simple terms, it means that a private person, or "whistleblower," brings a suit on behalf of the United States because that person has information that the defendant committed a crime. See U.S. Department of Justice, *False Claims Act Cases*.

improperly coded, which resulted in overpayment by the Medicare program.

The investigation was jointly conducted by the FBI, the OIG, and Texas Medicaid Fraud Control Unit. In the settlement, Dr. Marquez and other defendants agreed to pay the federal government and State of Texas a total of **$3,128,466.**[77]

2007 – Dr. Martin (Alabama)

Dr. Martin, a physician practicing in Alabama, pleaded guilty to healthcare fraud against the Medicare program and Blue Cross and Blue Shield of Alabama (BCBS). This case is particularly significant because it involved a joint investigation of claims submitted to both a federally funded healthcare program *and* a private insurer.

Dr. Martin, a general practitioner, was found to have fraudulently billed Medicare and BCBS, from 2001 to 2004, for services that were not provided to Medicare beneficiaries. Specifically, he billed for certain services under CPT code 14300, the surgical removal of malignant skin cancer tissue, when that specific procedure was not performed. In many instances, rather than removing cancerous tissue, Dr. Martin performed only simple procedures, such as removing noncancerous moles or warts, or other minor cosmetic procedures.

The plea agreement stipulated that Dr. Martin pay **$30,451.99** in restitution, **$600** in special assessments, and **$23,000** in costs of investigations and prosecution of the case, and he had to waive his appeal rights. Additionally, the physician agreed in a civil settlement to pay **$105,000** in restitution and to **permanently surrender his license to practice medicine**. Dr. Martin may also face imprisonment of not more than 10 years, an additional fine of **$250,000**, or both.

The U.S. Attorney stated, "Physicians are accountable for their bill-

[77] See U.S. Department of Justice, *U.S. Settles False Claims Act Suit.*

ing practices . . . Billing Medicare or private insurance companies for high priced services not rendered, drives up the costs in our health care system." Additionally, the FBI Special Agent in Charge, Birmingham Field Division, stated, "Investigations of health care fraud ensure accountability . . . accountability promotes honesty in billing practices." The investigation was conducted by the OIG along with the FBI.[78]

2007 – Dr. Francis and Nonphysician Staff (Florida)

This case is significant because **both physicians and nonphysicians** were investigated and charged for conspiracy to commit healthcare fraud related to improper billing practices. The defendants included Dr. Francis; the physician owner of a medical clinic located in Hialeah, Florida; a nonphysician office manager; and nonphysician medical assistants, among other defendants. Certain defendants were also charged with conspiracy to commit money laundering and substantive money laundering. The U.S. Attorney's Office filed a related criminal information charging Dr. Francis with one count of conspiracy to commit healthcare fraud. Dr. Francis agreed to waive indictment and plead guilty to the charges against him. As part of his agreement, Dr. Francis **voluntarily relinquished his medical license**.

According to the indictment, the co-defendants established a medical clinic, United Life Corp., which was used to defraud Medicare. Initially, the clinic saw various patients who were treated for a wide range of ailments and complaints. In or around September 2004, the clinic saw an influx of HIV patients, and eventually the clinic treated only HIV patients. From about January 2004 through about February 2005, United Life billed approximately $7,785,856 and received approximately $2,042,633 in Medicare reimbursements, based upon

[78] See U.S. Department of Justice, *Boaz Physician*.

claims for *alleged* treatments of intravenous immune globulin medications that purportedly were administered to the HIV patients.

The investigation was led by the FBI, the OIG's Miami Field Office, the DHHS OIG, and the Florida Department of Law Enforcement.[79]

2006 – Dr. Fica (Connecticut)

The U.S. entered into a civil settlement agreement with Dr. Fica, a Connecticut physician, for his alleged violation of FCA by submitting false claims to the Medicare and Medicaid programs. The complaint alleged that from 1996 to 2003, Dr. Fica employed Mr. Nakouzi, a nonphysician, to work at his medical practice. Mr. Nakouzi was not licensed to practice medicine, yet he treated patients.

Along, with various allegations of healthcare fraud, Dr. Fica billed insurance companies for services provided by Mr. Nakouzi and represented them as services provided by a physician. A complaint was filed under the qui tam "whistleblower" provision of the FCA, and it made several allegations about the propriety of Dr. Fica's billing practices.

On August 9, 2006, Dr. Fica was sentenced to **18 months in prison**, followed by **two years of supervised release**, for conspiring to commit healthcare fraud. He was also ordered to pay a fine of **$4,000** and nearly **$156,000** in criminal restitution. He additionally settled the civil suit for **$160,000**.

Mr. Nakouzi, the nonphysician employee, was sentenced to **two months in prison**, **four months of home confinement**, and **three years of supervised release**. He was ordered to pay a fine of only **$4,000** and perform **150 hours** of community service.

The investigations were jointly conducted by the Health Care Fraud Task Force (which is coordinated by the FBI and the OIG), the

---

[79] See U.S. Department of Justice, *Former U.S. Bureau of Prisons Staff Physician.*

Medicaid Fraud Control Unit, and the Connecticut Attorney General's office.[80]

2005 – Dr. McCarus (Maryland)

Dr. McCarus, a physician practicing in Towson, Maryland, was charged with FCA violations arising from submitting false claims for payment to Medicare, the Federal Health Employees Health Benefits Program (FHEHBP), and TRICARE. The complaint sought damages of nearly **$600,000** plus penalties ranging from **$5,500 to $11,000** for *each* of the **267 alleged false claims** submitted by the physician.

Among many other details, Dr. McCarus allegedly billed for the treatment of various cosmetic conditions, as if the treatments were covered medical services—when, in fact, they were noncovered, non-reimbursable services. He also allegedly engaged in a pattern of falsely diagnosing patients with reimbursable medical conditions, to make it appear as if the treatment were a covered service. For certain procedures, the complaint alleged that Dr. McCarus grossly and fraudulently inflated the size of the skin area that he said he treated in order to substantially increase his reimbursement under certain CPT codes.

The U.S. Attorney stated, "Doctors who defraud the federal health plans are cheating all taxpayers. The False Claims Act allows us to hold them accountable by recovering triple the amount of damages, plus additional penalties." The investigation was conducted by the Department of Health and Human Services OIG and Office of Personnel Management OIG.[81]

---

[80] See U.S. Department of Justice, *Waterbury Doctor*.

[81] See U.S. Department of Justice, *Complaint Filed Against Towson Doctor*.

How Investigations and Lawsuits Come About

Whistleblowers

Most often, investigations of the propriety of a medical practice's coding and billing practices are sparked by private persons, also known as "whistleblowers" or "relators," who initiate qui tam lawsuits against alleged perpetrators. The FCA explicitly permits anyone to file a lawsuit if that person (a) knows that an individual or organization is submitting false claims (of any kind) to the federal government and (b) has information that the defendant knowingly submitted, or caused the submission of, false or fraudulent claims to any federally funded program (including Medicare and Medicaid, among several others). With medical practices, the whistleblower is often a professional or administrative employee of the practice, a competitor, a patient, or any other person who has knowledge about the medical practice's billing practices. Quite often, the whistleblower is disgruntled for some reason.

According to the FCA, whistleblowers do not have to have been personally harmed by the defendant's conduct, and if the whistleblowers participated in the fraud themselves, that doesn't prevent them from bringing a lawsuit. As an incentive for whistleblowers to spark investigations, the FCA promises that they can share 15% to 25% of any monies the government recovers, if the government joins in the lawsuit, and up to 30% if the government decides not to intervene.

If the whistleblowers participated in the fraud, and a court finds that they planned or initiated the fraud, the court may reduce their award. Additionally, if whistleblowers are convicted of criminal action in connection with the fraud, they will not be awarded any monies.

Whistleblower rewards are often sizable, primarily because the FCA permits the government to recover treble (three times) damages for monies lost as a result of FCA violations. As previously mentioned, cases often settle for significant amounts before going to trial, but the settlements are typically less than three times the government's loss. The procedural aspects of whistleblower lawsuits are discussed in greater detail later in this chapter.

Recovery Audit Contractors (RACs)

The Centers for Medicare and Medicaid Services (CMS) initiated the Recovery Audit Contractor (RAC) Demonstration Program in 2007. Its purpose was to determine whether the use of RACs (i.e., private auditors under contract with the government) would be a cost-effective way to ensure that correct payments are made to providers.[82] In 2006, Congress made the RAC program permanent. Over the past three years, RACs have returned more than $300 million to the federal government from private audits conducted in three states. What concerns many is that a larger, national RAC Program, covering private audits by RACs, was rolled out in 19 states in the spring of 2008. In October 2008, five additional states will be added.[83]

RACs have a significant financial incentive to participate in private audits because the RAC Program permits them to keep approximately 20% of any overpayments. Among numerous critics of the RAC Program, Don May, vice president for policy at the American Hospital Association, described the program as follows: "What we have here is bureaucrats and government contractors coming in and trying to second guess what doctors and nurses have done . . . They're playing Monday morning quarterback."[84]

The Office of Management and Budget (OMB) estimates that Medicare payment errors total approximately $10.8 billion per year. It's estimated that approximately 4.5 million Medicare claims are filed each

---

[82] Centers for Medicare and Medicaid Services, *Recovery Audit Contractor Overview.*

[83] Freking, "Audits Sting Hospitals, Physicians."

[84] Ibid.

work day, and 9,579 claims are filed per minute.[85] While it would be a logistical and financial nightmare for the government to review each and every claim filed, the OIG and government contractors review a fraction of these claims.

RACs are engaged to find both overpayments and underpayments; they've returned approximately $20 million in underpayments to providers, but the amount of monies returned to the federal government through the Demonstration Program is astonishing. One CMS report shows that RACs reviewed more than 900 million claims in Florida, California, and New York during the Program's first two and a half years, and they identified errors in less than 0.2% of the claims reviewed.[86]

Qui Tam ("Whistleblower") Litigation

This section provides a brief overview of qui tam litigation under the FCA. Additional information can be obtained on the Department of Justice's website (www.doj.gov), from the statutory text of the FCA, or by consulting an attorney.[87]

By law, a qui tam complaint must be "filed under seal," which means that all records relating to the case must be kept on a secret docket by the court, and they are not publicly available for 60 days or longer while the government investigates the allegations and decides whether to join the lawsuit. Investigations are often conducted jointly by the U.S. Department of Health and Human Services, Office of Inspector General (OIG), Department of Justice (DOJ), and Federal Bureau of Investigation (FBI) as well as other federal and/or state law enforcement agencies. After 60 days, if it wants the case to remain un-

---

[85] Ibid.

[86] Ibid.

[87] For a brief overview of qui tam litigation, see U.S. Department of Justice, *False Claims Act Cases*.

der seal, the DOJ must file a motion with the judge showing "good cause" why the case should remain under seal. Typically, the DOJ requests an extension of the seal for six months at a time.

A whistleblower must also file a "disclosure statement" with the DOJ, which contains substantially all the evidence about the allegations that the whistleblower possesses. This disclosure statement is not filed in any court, and it's not available to the defendant. Under the FCA, the local DOJ attorney (U.S. Attorney) must "diligently" investigate the allegations. This investigation usually involves one or more of the law enforcement agencies mentioned earlier. Copies of the complaint are given only to the DOJ, including the U.S. Attorney, and to the assigned judge of the district court.

The investigation often involves subpoenas for documents or electronic records, witness interviews, compelled oral testimony from one or more individuals or organizations, and consultations with experts. If there's a parallel criminal investigation of the physician's practice, search warrants and other criminal investigation tools may be used to obtain evidence as well.

At the investigation's conclusion, the DOJ may choose to join in, decline to intervene in, move to dismiss, or settle the whistleblower's claim. If the DOJ intervenes, it often files its own complaint setting forth its statement of the facts and the relief sought. The DOJ may also assert additional claims arising under other statutes (such as the Truth in Negotiation Act, the Public Contracts Anti-Kickback Act, or common law) that a private citizen would not be entitled to assert. Once the accused physician and/or other defendants are served with a copy of the government's complaint, each named defendant is required to file an answer within 20 days.[88]

Bringing a qui tam lawsuit isn't an easy decision to make, based on the detailed process for filing the claim as well as the possible ripple

[88] U.S. Department of Justice, *False Claims Act Cases.*

effect on the whistleblower's personal and professional life. But this type of lawsuit is becoming an increasingly common way to report purported healthcare fraud. There are various reasons for this, including the potential for significant financial rewards, moral and ethical obligations, and the job protection that's guaranteed to whistleblowers under the FCA. The law provides a 10-year statute of limitations on claims brought under the FCA.

Chapter 25

Avoiding Liability under the Federal False Claims Act

Invited Chapter
Erum Raza, Esq.

As discussed in the last chapter, generally speaking, the False Claims Act (FCA) can subject physicians to significant civil monetary penalties and criminal liability as well as loss of their medical license. Such penalties may be imposed for improperly submitting claims for reimbursement to any federally funded healthcare program—including Medicare, Medicaid, or TRICARE—whether or not the claims were submitted intentionally, and provided that they were submitted in violation of the FCA. This chapter discusses (a) the measures physicians can take to ensure that their medical practices comply with the FCA, (b) the importance of responding to an audit or investigation in a prompt manner, and (c) the ethical considerations of coding and billing.

Protecting Your Practice: Quality Control and Risk Assessment

Although there's no way to completely insulate your practice—and, specifically, your coding and billing practices—from a government investigation, there are several prudent steps that physicians and practice managers should keep in mind:

1. Select persons or entities that perform the practice's billing functions extremely carefully and with caution. As discussed previously, physicians can be held responsible for false claims submitted on their behalf, even if they weren't aware of it.
2. Supervise, on an ongoing basis, all persons or entities performing the billing function.
3. Perform routine *in-house* audits of charts and claim submissions for completeness, accuracy, and medical necessity.
4. Make sure all billing personnel are aware of, and comply with, all government regulations for filing claims.
5. Encourage employees to report mistakes, questions, concerns, and wrongdoings of any kind related to the coding and billing functions to you and other managers.
6. As soon as a problem is detected, take immediate action to prevent similar mistakes or further wrongdoing.
7. Provide clearly written and adequate documentation of all services and procedures provided.
8. Provide adequate *formal* training (or access to formal training) to all office personnel involved in billing, at *any level*, to make them well versed in CPT coding and processes.
9. Engage outside experts, consultants, and attorneys to periodically review and audit your billing policies and procedures before they're scrutinized.
10. Avoid routine coding. Treat every patient encounter as

unique—i.e., avoid coding every clinic visit with the same evaluation and management codes, when some are clearly less complex than others.

11. Avoid upcoding (e.g., replacing the most appropriate code with a more complex service or procedure code). This is unethical and, regardless of intention, can be investigated by the Office of Inspector General (OIG).
12. Avoid unbundling, which is defined in the *National Correct Coding Policy Manual* as "the billing of multiple procedure codes for a group of procedures that are covered by a single comprehensive code"[89] (i.e., dividing one service into distinct or component parts and coding each distinct part as if it were a separate service; or reporting individual codes for related services when one comprehensive code includes all related services).
13. Avoid providing and billing for unnecessary services. If there's no overall benefit to the patient that outweighs the risk, inconvenience, or cost of the service or procedure, it's medically unnecessary—and it's unethical to knowingly provide such service or procedure for financial gain.[90]
14. Seek written instructions from local Medicare carriers, the American Medical Association (AMA) Department of Coding and Nomenclature, or Health Care Financing Administration (HCFA) if you have doubts about the appropriateness of your coding policies and procedures.

---

[89] Centers for Medicare and Medicaid Services, *National Correct Coding Initiatives.*

[90] See American College of Physicians, *Ethics Manual.* See also Riddick, *The Code of Medical Ethics.*

Responding to an Audit/Investigation

Be advised that a delay in responding to an investigatory inquiry or complaint can ultimately prejudice a physician's ability to resolve a case favorably. If you or your practice becomes the subject of an investigation, immediately secure a qualified attorney who can prepare and assist in your defense in a timely manner and engage a medical billing expert (MBE).

MBEs can testify, if necessary, as to the medical necessity and reimbursability, under existing Medicare guidelines, of the services and diagnostic tests at issue. MBEs can also testify about the adequacy and appropriateness of your medical record documentation, coding, billing records, practices, policies, and procedures. Personal notes and conclusions may carry less weight than a qualified MBE's testimony. A prudent step would be to engage a qualified MBE to prepare a report to solidify your defense and expedite dismissal of an FCA case as quickly as possible. Share this report, and/or an independent MBE's opinion about the billing issues in question, with the U.S. Attorney investigating your practice.

Hurdles Facing Physicians with Respect to Accurate Coding

In recent years, accurate coding has become increasingly challenging for various reasons. To say the least, national coding policies are ambiguous. Current Procedural Terminology (CPT) codes and policies are complex and hard to grasp for many physicians and their billing personnel. Correct use of CPT codes requires extensive experience and training. Certification in physician coding services is offered by organizations such as the American Academy of Professional Coders and the American Health Information Management Association, and many consulting companies provide seminars on changes to the CPT system. However, billing personnel often don't have adequate experience and training. Given the increased scrutiny in this area, physicians should make sure they engage skilled personnel to handle their coding and billing function and stay up to date on regularly published clarifications of coding policy, such as AMA's CPT Assistant. Physicians and billing personnel should also familiarize themselves with major government initiatives, such as HCFA's *National Correct Coding Policy Manual.*

Ethical Principles with Respect to Coding

Physicians have widely complained that reduced compensation for services over the years is patently unfair. While this is a legitimate concern, inappropriate or aggressive coding is not a legal solution. The federal government has made explicitly clear that it will not tolerate healthcare fraud at any level. One way to deal with the problem of reduced compensation is to provide additional legitimate services to patients and to focus on more careful, but accurate, coding of legitimate services.

Several professional societies have specifically addressed the ethics of proper coding, and they've concluded that physicians have numerous ethical obligations pertaining to their coding practices.[91] To summarize, keep in mind these general ethical principles:

- **Nonmalficence** – Physicians have an obligation to not harm the patient. Unnecessary services can result in physical harm to patients by exposing them to unnecessary risk. Additionally, inappropriate coding can result in financial harm to patients, because by increasing physician revenue, out-of-pocket expenses for patients may also increase.
- **Veracity** – Physicians are obligated to deal honestly with

[91] See American College of Physicians, *American College of Physicians Ethics Manual*; American Health Information Management Association, *Standards of Ethical Coding*; Riddick, *The Code of Medical Ethics.*

patients and colleagues. Any coding practice that misrepresents services provided violates this obligation.

- **Justice** – The physician is entitled to receive only payments that are just. Inappropriate or inaccurate coding to increase revenue beyond what's normally provided for a given service is not just.

Be an Advocate

There's no doubt that physicians have an ethical duty to file accurate claims for reimbursement, and many physicians have advocated ethical coding and billing practices. But many argue that *insurers* have not acknowledged their responsibility to do the same and have not made strides to minimize unnecessary complexity, routine delay in reimbursements, and routine inappropriate denials of claims.

Insurers' ethical obligation to promptly reimburse for claims is equal to physicians' obligations to promptly submit claims when services have been properly rendered, accurately coded, and billed. Physicians should reach out to their local chapters of medical specialty societies, Medicare carrier advisory committees, state insurance commissioners, and state agencies that regulate managed care organizations. This is a way to place increased pressure on insurers to comply with their ethical responsibility.

About the Guest Author

Erum Raza is a corporate attorney and associate in the Princeton, New Jersey, office of Fox Rothschild LLP. Her corporate and tax practice focuses on various issues relating to professional service practices, closely held businesses, and the purchase and sale of businesses. She is admitted to practice in New Jersey and New York, and she specializes in healthcare law and business transactions. Prior to law school, Ms.

Raza was a senior tax associate at Andersen LLP's New York City office, where she focused on federal and state tax compliance and consulting for public and private corporations, partnerships, limited liability companies, and other business organizations. Ms. Raza is also a CPA admitted to practice in New York. For questions or for more information, please contact her at eraza@foxrothschild.com or visit www.foxrothschild.com.

Part V

Electronic Medical Records and SOAP Notes

The adventures first . . . explanations take such a dreadful time.

—The Gryphon
Alice's Adventures in Wonderland
Lewis Carroll

Well-managed medical records and SOAP notes bring two key values to both patients and practice owners: better healthcare and lower audit risk. A solid note management discipline is entirely dependent on internal practice management processes. Therefore, EMR and SOAP notes belong to a "pre-network effect" service category, designed to deliver value to practice owners independently of the number of practices using the Vericle network. Efficiency then becomes the key challenge of EMR and SOAP notes—but what is the best way to implement them to deliver their values most efficiently, without adding costs?

A recent article in the New York Times ("Most Doctors Aren't Using Electronic Health Records") cited an interesting and conflicting observation: on one hand, doctors who use electronic health records (EHR) say overwhelmingly that such records have helped improve the quality and timeliness of care. On the other hand, fewer than one in five of the nation's doctors have started using such records. Most doctors in private practice, especially small practices, lack the financial incentive to invest in computerized records. In fact, only 8.6% of small practices (1–3 doctors) have started using EHR, as compared with 50% of large practices (more than 50 doctors).[92]

The key reason for slow EHR adoption rates seem to be economic: providers, already squeezed for reimbursement by the payers, lack the financial incentive to make a significant investment in EHR—often as high as $20,000 per doctor—and undergo the painful and costly conversion process from paper. Experts agree that EHR would be adopted faster in a consumer-driven healthcare system, where innovation benefits the entrepreneurial provider. In the absence of a consumer-driven healthcare market, the government—i.e., the taxpayers—subsidize technological progress, shifting the system selection and pricing decisions from healthcare providers to bureaucrats.

That decision making today isn't easy: 54% of doctors without EHR said that not being able to find an electronic health record that met their needs was a "major barrier" to adoption.[93] Why can't doctors find products that meet their needs in a market saturated with 400 EMR vendors? Is it because these products tend to be designed for hospitals—big customers—instead of small practices?

The same article concludes with this: "'Do I see more patients because of this technology? Probably no,' Dr. Masucci said. 'But I am doing a better job with the patients I am seeing. It almost forces you to

---

[92] Lohr, "Most Doctors."

[93] Ibid.

be a better doctor.'"[94] Is it reasonable to expect a technology to force you to become a better doctor or see more patients a day? Does the number of patients per day adequately measure healthcare quality or even productivity?

In a consumer-driven market, fewer patients would visit a practice that lacks modern documentation processes, and more doctors would develop realistic business-driven requirements for EMR. The market would guide the EMR vendors, and the process of EMR adoption would become much easier in terms of matching functionality, convenient conversion process, and affordable pricing.

Part V contains five chapters about EMR and SOAP notes. Chapter 26 outlines requirements for intelligent notes. Chapter 27 presents the challenges and solutions for integrating best-of-breed EMR and billing technologies. Chapter 28 discusses physician interface issues in EMR and billing systems and presents five ways to resolve them. Chapter 29 compares dictation with point-and-click user interface. This chapter was contributed by Eric Fishman, MD, who practiced orthopedic surgery for over 20 years prior to creating *EHR Scope*, a quarterly publication that includes the largest compendium of EMR software. Chapter 30 concludes Part V by presenting a concept of integrating practice management, electronic health records, and billing services into a unified platform. This chapter was contributed by Joseph Kamelgard, MD, who uses his combined background in medical surgery and biomedical engineering to provide 21st-century tools to clinicians so they can deliver appropriate medical care to their patients while remaining profitable.

---

[94] Ibid.

Chapter 26

Intelligent SOAP Notes

Doctors and therapists must produce clinical documentation in ever-increasing volume and detail to ensure the best healthcare, get medical claims paid in full and on time, and protect the practice from post-payment audits and unfair litigation.

But the speed of completing visit documentation conflicts with documentation accuracy and thoroughness. For insurance companies, patient visit documentation must be precise and comprehensive. If the quality of documentation is high, the medical billing appeals on unpaid claims are paid faster and at a higher rate. Otherwise, appeals are denied and the practice becomes vulnerable to post-payment audits, refunds, and penalties.

Insurance companies don't care how long it takes to produce good documentation. But for the provider, slow documentation impedes practice profitability and wastes valuable time. The doctor must be done with visit documentation by the time the patient leaves the office.

To ensure comprehensive note coverage, the healthcare industry adopted a two-pronged approach. First, the doctor uses the SOAP notes format, which reflects four key stages of patient care—Subjective observations, Objective symptoms, diagnostic Assessment, and the treatment Plan:

1. **Subjective** – The initial portion of the SOAP note format consists of subjective observations. These are symptoms typically expressed verbally by the patient. They include the patient's descriptions of pain or discomfort, the presence of nausea or dizziness, or other descriptions of dysfunction.

2. **Objective** – The next part of the format includes symptoms that can actually be measured, seen, heard, touched, felt, or smelled. Included in objective observations are vital signs such as temperature, pulse, respiration, skin color, swelling, and the results of diagnostic tests.

3. **Assessment** – Assessment is the diagnosis of the patient's condition based on subjective observations and objective symptoms. In some cases, the diagnosis may be a simple determination, while in other cases, it may include multiple diagnosis possibilities.

4. **Plan** – The last part of the SOAP note is the treatment plan, which may include laboratory and/or radiological tests ordered for the patient, medications ordered, treatments performed (e.g., minor surgical procedures), patient referrals (sending the patient to a specialist), patient disposition (e.g., home care, bed rest, short-term or long-term disability, days excused from work, admission to the hospital), and follow-up directions for the patient.

Next, each of the four key SOAP stages consists of templates reflecting multiple possibilities for each stage. Templates, organized according to SOAP order, ensure comprehensive coverage and allow the doctor to simply check multiple selection boxes on a screen that's driven by a computer program.

Templates have attracted twofold criticism, from both the provider and the payer sides. The providers dislike the lack of built-in intelligence to reflect an individual doctor's preferences to treat patients. The payers often suspect low-quality template-generated notes and poor reflection of a patient's true state and treatment progress, because of a template's susceptibility to mechanical clicking and difficulty of interpretation.

The challenge is to combine the advantages of template and verbal formats, and avoid their shortcomings, to describe precise patient conditions, ensure productive medical billing, prepare for regulatory scrutiny, and improve practice productivity. To overcome the perception of mechanically generated notes while saving the doctor typing time, some vendors have created specialized products that use randomized wording for each template. Such automatically generated notes include sentence structures that closely resemble natural speech patterns.

Flexibility and integration must be key design features of SOAP notes. In the opening section, for example, you create new patient files that grow organically with each visit or treatment. Built-in intelligence allows you to customize a document to your own preferences and observe the entire patient progress history in a single screen. Integrating the native system with medical billing systems enables automated claim generation, validation, and submission to payers for payment.

SOAP notes must not merely emulate the paper folder that every doctor has for every patient. They must use computer technology to help automate routine tasks and create a faster, easier, and error-free process to increase practice profitability and reduce audit risks.

Chapter 27

Best-of-Breed Billing Plus EMR – Transition Challenges and Integration Plan

The limited choice between mediocre full-scope products and excellent single-function systems has been expanding in step with the increasing reliability of Internet technology and standardization of system interfaces.

"An integrated best-of-breed product helps patient care and clinical error reduction, financial performance, and regulatory compliance," says Boris Petrikovsky, MD, PhD, chairman of the Department of Obstetrics & Gynecology at Nassau University Medical Center and professor of Obstetrics, Gynecology, and Reproductive Medicine at Stony Brook University School of Medicine.

Comprehensive, integrated best-of-breed solutions that combine modern EMR software and billing service can be used under the "pay as you go" business model. The SaaS (Software as a Service) model allows physicians to confirm the benefits of technology solutions first and pay later. While such solutions deliver multiple risk management and operations control benefits, they also pose significant transition challenges.

Integrated SaaS and Outsourced Service

Improved operations control, risk avoidance, and added revenue are the most significant benefits of integrated outsourced and SaaS solutions during both implementation and exploitation phases:

- SaaS requires no large up-front investment in hardware, software licenses, or systems integration on the part of the user.
- SaaS shifts the onus of systems management from the user to the SaaS vendor.

In business accounting terms, SaaS turns capital expense into operating expense, which translates into the following:

- A better balance sheet
- Lower risk, especially during the period of rapid technology innovation on one hand and practice-building stages on the other hand

Transition – People and Processes

Once you've selected your outsourced solution vendor(s) for EMR and billing, you face a transition challenge. This involves people, processes, and technology. Since the SaaS model eliminates traditional systems management headaches, you can focus on only people and processes:

1. **Communicate, communicate, communicate** – The likelihood of a successful implementation is directly proportional to staff involvement. Review current workflow, understand expected changes, and make sure everybody in the

practice agrees with them, including the practice manager, doctors, and office personnel. To avoid errors and conflicts in the future, leave nobody behind using the old workflow. Document the following:

a. **Steps** required to schedule an appointment: register a patient's arrival; find out an outstanding balance; bring the patient to the exam room; find previous diagnostics, treatment, and financial plans; and gather vital signs, medication, and allergy lists.
b. **Tasks** required to get paid in full and on time. Include coding, claim submission, denial review, appeals, follow-up with payers and patients, secondary submissions, and a review of accounts receivable.
c. **Individuals** performing those tasks, locations, and task durations.

2. **Manage expectations** – Laurence J. Peter observed in *The Peter Principle*, "If you don't know where you are going, you will probably end up somewhere else." Document specific changes in the new workflow. Identify specific steps in the new workflow that require fewer or less-qualified resources. Quantify expected benefits in terms of saved resources, added revenue, and personnel savings. Schedule specific timelines for meeting specific financial benchmarks.

3. **Control the fear of change** – Don't force the new system onto the old workflow. If the old processes had met practice business requirements, you wouldn't have looked for better solutions. Carefully design the new workflow, leveraging the new solutions together with workflow partici-

pants, including the practice manager and every doctor.

4. **Prioritize** – Don't try to implement an entirely new process that includes all new features at once. Soften the transition shock by using a gradual approach, minimizing the amount of changes, but maintaining a steady and sufficiently frequent pace of small changes to complete the transition on time. Avoid scheduling migration to a new system coincidental with the practice move to a new physical location.

5. **Lead** – Without a manager for the entire transition process, members of the transition team will find other priorities and won't take responsibility for delivery. While a technical background or prior familiarity with EMR is helpful, the following leadership skills and a commitment to accomplish results are critical for successful implementation:
   a. Communication
   b. Expectations management
   c. Consensus building and conflict resolution
   d. Delegation
   e. Attention to detail
   f. Verification of delivery

6 **Track** – Schedule regular (weekly) implementation review meetings with the practice manager to do one of the following:
   a. Ascertain that progress is made according to the plan
   b. Modify the plan

7. **Schedule** – Without specific action items, including spe-

cific owners and delivery dates, implementation will drag on and exceed allocated costs. Consider using a process tracking system (e.g., TrackLogix). Pay special attention to the following:

a. **Payer enrollments** – Fill out required paperwork. Check for clerical errors.
b. **SOAP note customization** – Review current notes. Consult every doctor in the practice when designing the new templates.
c. **Custom reporting** – Address any unique practice needs.
d. **Legacy systems and data** – Review interfaces. Contact vendors. Prioritize record upload.
e. **Testing** – Design a test plan for specific transition and integration items. Schedule dates.
f. **Going live** – Find low-volume days to reduce damage from unexpected errors.
g. **Personnel training** – Focus on the new process. Test newly acquired system skills.

8. **Train gradually** – Allocate enough time to train everybody on both the new processes and the technology. Don't try to jam everything your system can do into a single training session. Expect multiple training sessions, adjusting to the participants' learning pace. Ease in, and use the "onion peel" approach, training personnel on only those features required for the new processes and specific scheduled items on hand:

   a. **Basic scheduler and superbill** – Learn to schedule patient appointments, enter demographics for a new patient, test patient eligibility and balance online, and enter charges for a patient visit.

b. **Workbench and problem tracking** – Identify denied claims. Respond to billing operations requests for information, review denied claims, and update claim data.
c. **EMR** – Update SOAP notes. Test drug interaction. Review referral reports.
d. **Basic accountability reports** – Track charges, payments, and billing quality (percent of A/R beyond 120 days). Generate a summary of accounts receivable by payer or a breakdown of revenue by physician for a given month or cumulative to date. Review end-of-day reports for patient visits, new patients, patient visit averages, missed appointments, and accounts receivable.
e. **Advanced EMR** – Modify SOAP note templates. Modify alert generation rules.
f. **Patient relationship management** – Create and track payment plans. Manage patient compliance.
g. **Advanced reporting and performance analysis** – Track payment variations by CPT codes and payers. Identify the worst payer for the best-revenue-producing CPT code. Analyze your audit risk exposure. Identify undercoded or overcoded claims.

Chapter 28

Physician Interface to EMR

Billing and claims management services and systems help healthcare providers manage the rising costs of healthcare as well as increase overall administrative efficiency. The wider the scope of solution, the more benefit it delivers to the practice. The most important scope enhancement in recent years is the addition of integrated electronic medical records (EMR) solutions, which is the heart of the medical practice-IT value chain. The comprehensive nature of EMR consolidates a patient's personal and administrative information, health history, prescriptions, treatments, and conditions. The ability of EMR to perform such data aggregation at the point of care elevates its benefit from merely recording a patient encounter to creating a useful decision support system.

The most critical part of any system is its interfaces to other systems and, especially, its human interface. Typically, EMR allows three kinds of input: typing, dictation, and point-and-click templates. Most physicians choose dictation over typing and point-and-click templates for reasons of convenience and time efficiencies.

While the preference of dictation over typing is obvious, recent technology progress and regulatory compliance pressures make point-

and-click templates superior to dictation.

Dictation and Transcription

Medical transcription saves time compared with handwritten notes or typing. It intuitively matches the physician's working style and power of personal expression, and it's easy to dictate using a phone, PDA, or dictation machine. Human transcribers or voice recognition systems transcribe the dictation into medical notes.

But transcription has multiple disadvantages:

- **Incompleteness** – If notes are not captured immediately at the point of care, it's too easy to exclude important details.
- **Costly processing** – Report generation using unstructured data is much more time-consuming and expensive.
- **Time delays for accessibility** – It typically takes 12 to 24 hours for chart turnaround.

Note incompleteness is the most important disadvantage of dictation and transcription, because comprehensive medical notes are key to surviving a post-payment insurance audit.

Point-and-Click Templates

A point-and-click template presents a selection of data elements, a navigation mechanism, and a point-and-click process for capturing patient information. The doctor simply points and clicks, selecting appropriate choices, while the system fills out a complete record of selections, which makes up the resulting encounter notes. Such a structured approach offers multiple benefits:

- **Consistency** – Structured data ensures note completeness and avoids missing important details. It enhances the ability to generate clinically useful reports, such as appointment reminders or disease management.
- **Customization** – The doctor specifies the template layout to precisely match the workflow of the practice.
- **Lower error rate** – Standardization of input precludes errors of omission or spelling.
- **Faster decision making** – Similar observations have similar notes, resulting in consistent decisions.
- **Immediate accessibility for processing** – Since notes are created within the EMR system, they're available immediately upon completion.

However, point-and-click data entry also has several disadvantages:

- **Complexity** – It takes more effort to create the notes using point-and-click templates than just writing or dictating.
- **Data entry time** – It may take too long to walk through all the required templates in front of the patient.
- **Cost** – As each practice has different workflows, template customization may be costly.

The added complexity of point-and-click templates is clearly justifiable because of guaranteed completeness, which is key to regulatory compliance and the ability to survive post-payment audits. The data entry time can also be reduced by allocating a lion's share of the doctor's time to comprehensive documentation during the initial examination, and then restricting the documentation scope during subsequent visits to note updates only. The structured nature of point-and-click templates is naturally conducive to such time prioritization.

Summary

Although some physicians prefer familiar over convenient, and convenient over better functionality, transcription must be viewed as an inferior component of the interface array to the modern EMR system; at most, transcription plays a complementary role to point-and-click templates. Modern physician office automation technologies combine billing and EMR features, and they provide both kinds of interfaces, adding to the efficacy and efficiency of practice workflow. Powerful Vericle-like technologies also facilitate rapid customization of point-and-click templates, optimizing the physician's interface to the EMR system, providing an added degree of regulatory compliance, and reducing post-payment audit risks.

Chapter 29

Narrative vs. Data: To Dictate or To Click?

Invited Chapter
Eric Fishman, MD

Electronic medical records are here to stay. Not only are there an increasing number of physicians using EMRs on a daily basis, there's also an incredible political push to increase their adoption to an even greater extent. A large number of advantages to patients, physicians, and the population in general occur from this migration to an electronic charting format. However, there are some disadvantages as well.

We'll discuss a few of these disadvantages, and then provide a readily available solution to many of them. All of these discussions will revolve around the "chart note."

Cookie-Cutter Templates

An oft-cited, but possibly rather trivial, disadvantage of electronic formats is the fact that the reports created are rather "cookie-cutter" sounding. While the patients who arrive in the medical practice have an infinite variety of presentations, the reports discussing them all sound pretty much the same. Yes—some patients have "severe pain" while others have "moderate pain," some have "severe restriction in range of motion" while others have "moderate restriction in range of motion." But the reports, in general, look, feel, and seem to be about the same patient—rather than about the unique person who presented as *your* patient.

Templates can be used to very quickly produce voluminous documentation on patients. But do they really document the medical encounter, or do they merely repeat what the EMR programmers think patients' presentations consist of? In many instances, it clearly appears as if the latter is the case.

Cloning – and Errors

A related objection to the use of templates is that it's rather easy for physicians to document "facts" that were not part of the patient encounter. For instance, we've all heard of the medical student who writes "PERRLA" when the patient has a glass eye. However, this occurs not because of a "transcription error," but rather because the student didn't really look for papillary accommodation in both eyes.

This concept has now been put on steroids in many physicians' medical reporting habits. Once a template, or trigger, has been chosen, it's easier to leave it intact than to modify it. Thus, if you've tested, for instance, the biceps and triceps reflexes, you might choose the template "upper extremity reflexes are normal." This might lead to a sentence such as "The biceps, triceps, and brachioradialis reflexes are all normal." But many physicians don't test the brachioradialis, therefore this inaccuracy would be placed into the record not by conscious effort on the part of the physician, but rather by a cumbersome system that attempts to streamline the documentation process—and sometimes does so too efficiently. This is merely one possible trivial example of an "imposed error"—but we're all familiar with the extensive review of symptoms (ROS) in physicians' notes, when we clearly understand that neither the physician, nor the staff, nor even the patients themselves have addressed these issues before or during the patient encounter.

Efficiency

A possibly more significant disadvantage of this sea change in documentation methodology is the increasing amount of time that it takes to record a patient encounter. Chapter 28, for instance, notes "data entry time" as one of the disadvantages of point-and-click data entry, and trying to minimize this time is a very important part of successful EMR implementations. In no other industry are the highest-paid and most-skillful workers asked to become stenographers, completing their own paperwork. Attorneys have legal secretaries, and bankers have executive assistants. But in 2008, physicians are being asked to complete, by themselves, the extraordinary amount of paperwork required to properly document a patient encounter. They're used to dictating, usually very quickly, and having someone else perform the labor-intensive task of getting those dictated words onto paper—and as a general rule, they're not happy about changing that paradigm.

Because of this, the EMR adoption rate is lagging. We hear, not infrequently, of large-scale implementations in which one or more physicians actually leave the medical facility because of their displeasure with the new electronic medical record system. It usually isn't that physicians don't want to "use" the system, but rather that they don't want to take on the extra burden of creating their documentation.

Speech Recognition to the Rescue

All of these disadvantages, however, can be easily overcome with the judicious use of speech recognition software. At first thought, you might consider it most appropriate to dictate the entire report, as in the "old style," and then just copy and paste it into the electronic medical record. However, for a variety of reasons, this is not an appropriate solution.

One reason is that doing a "copy and paste" into the EMR won't allow you to take advantage of the proper use of templates to speed appropriate documentation. Much thought has been given to methods of improving medical reporting—and if you don't use these templates or macros for such features as the ROS, in an intellectually honest and ethical fashion, you're missing out on some of the more powerful and beneficial features of an EMR.

More importantly, you need to consider one of the critical reasons that politicians, for example, are interested in EMRs: "data." Speech recognition can produce a very fine "narrative" report. However, it doesn't permit data mining, and it isn't consistent with interoperable medical records. It's the interoperability of medical records that many feel is so important, and without a standardized structure to the record, this opportunity is lost. It is this interoperability that will, by some estimates, save $77 billion annually in healthcare costs.[95]

Another advantage of data capture is improving the healthcare of an individual physician's patients. An obvious example is when a medication has been recalled, such as what occurred with Vioxx. With "data," it's rather easy to contact each patient who has ever received a prescription or sample of that medicine. However, with only "narratives," it becomes much more difficult to accomplish this objective.

---

[95] Ball and Gold, "Banking on Health."

So, What Is the Ideal Solution?

The ideal marriage between data and narratives exists when a physician uses a speech recognition software program, such as Dragon NaturallySpeaking Medical, to dictate a few sentences—or even a paragraph or two of history—and then uses the standard point-and-click method for the more standardized portions of the report, such as medications, past medical history, and physical examination. Then, the physician can use speech recognition again to offer thought processes for portions of the assessment and plan. This allows for the greatest capture of data and the most readable report—and it is, I believe, the ideal solution at this point in time.

You should note that when dictating the history, for instance, you can speed up the process even further by using voice macros. These shortcuts allow you to enter meaningful amounts of text, but still speak the variables that are so important in the patient history.

Report Production

When a patient enters a physician's office and a history is taken, the physician should dictate the narrative history using some of the patient's own words. This can be done with a wireless microphone that can be relatively unobtrusive. The physician can use a stylus to click through most of the ROS, PMH (past medical history), FH (family history), and probably even PE (physical examination). When the physician reaches the assessment and plan, it's preferable to once again start dictating so that the physician's actual thought process can be understood.

Summary

To take the best advantage of modern EMR technology, a judicious combination of speaking and clicking can produce the most readable, cost-effective, defensible, and accurate medical records—while minimizing the degradation of data capture that's so important in the modern medical office.

About the Guest Author

Eric Fishman, MD, practiced orthopedic surgery for over 20 years—first in Caribou, Maine, and later in West Palm Beach, Florida. Dr. Fishman's company, 1450 Inc., is the world's largest distributor of Dragon NaturallySpeaking Medical software. His publication, *EHR Scope*, includes the largest compendium of EMR software, and through his website (www.EMRConsultant.com), he has provided recommendations to thousands of practices concerning their health information technology. Having spent over a decade integrating speech recognition into various electronic medical record software programs, he's considered a world expert in the use of speech recognition in medical records production.

Chapter 30

Integrating Practice Management, Electronic Health Records, and Billing Services

Invited Chapter
Joseph Kamelgard, MD, FACS

In this chapter, I shall present the concept of integrating practice management, electronic health records, and billing services into a unified platform. Having been in clinical practice for 10 years myself, I became quite familiar with the shortcomings of fragmented work flow, and I found that this is a common problem that plagues many practices. This could be the result of a decentralized practice environment with a call center in one location and multiple clinical offices, or simply one clinical office and an outsourced billing service. Whatever the scenario, when the work flow is segmented across multiple locations and/or processes, menial tasks such as data entry require redundant efforts—and these can introduce errors that affect the quality of the healthcare delivered and typically cause the fiscal bottom line to suffer.

This fragmented work flow is the traditional way in which medicine has been practiced over the years. However, the medical economics of the 21st century, with decreasing reimbursements and the need for increased accountability, require healthcare providers to increase their efficiency if they want to remain profitable. One of the most dramatic changes taking place in medical offices, hospitals, and other healthcare facilities today is the implementation of electronic patient management (PM) and electronic health record (EHR) systems. The time of the "appointment book" and the "paper chart" is rapidly coming to an end. As a matter of fact, there are government programs that currently reward those already switching to the electronic realm. Soon, there will be punishments in the form of fines for those who don't make the switch. Within the not-too-distant future, it will likely be mandated by law that all medicine be practiced electronically.

Literally hundreds of vendors and products have come to market in an attempt to provide clinicians with the proper tools to approach the huge task of moving from the old to the new way of practicing medicine. No one solution can fit every scenario like a cookie cutter. As a result, different vendors have taken different directions in their product development. Some products are stand-alone (referred to as a client server); others are services accessed over the Internet (called either an application service provider [ASP] or Software as a Service [SaaS]). Others still might offer some hybrid of these two. Some products provide only PM solutions, others provide only EHR services, while a number of vendors offer both PM and EHR solutions in one software suite, with varying degrees of integration.

A good PM system enables a practice to become much more time efficient with all of its routine tasks. This may start with patient appointment scheduling—functioning like an electronic version of an appointment book, but adding the functionality of registration, insurance validation, reminder phone calls, balance checking, satisfaction surveys, etc. A good PM system should integrate with an EHR in a way that allows bi-directional transferring of information relevant to both systems.

Consider these requirements when choosing a PM product:

1. Find a product that can perform all of the practice's current tasks.
2. Look for ease of implementation and use (i.e., the user interface should be intuitive and require little training).
3. Ensure that the product is expandable and customizable, so you can adapt to the future needs of the practice.
4. Be certain that there's seamless integration between the PM and EHR components for the bi-directional transfer of information.

A good EHR has the capability to focus on an individual medical specialty, creating separate, deep, and specialty-specific knowledge bases. The EHR should be able to adapt to the practice's own work flow and not require the practice to comply with the EHR's predetermined work flow. Another important feature is the customizability of the user and work flow interfaces at the individual practice level. It's important to know if this can be done and, if yes, whether it can be done by the practice or if it requires vendor intervention (which typically adds cost). Probably the most important features any clinician would want from an EHR are the capabilities to back up patient records and establish a disaster recovery plan. This last point is vital to the practice and can't be overemphasized.

Consider these requirements when choosing an EHR product:

1. Find a product that can handle your area of specialization without encumbering you with data items from other specialties.
2. Look for an EHR product that can adapt to your individual

practice habits.

3. Ensure that your patient records are accessible 24/7/365.
4. Be certain that there's frequent automatic data backup.
5. Only consider an EHR product with a readily available and easy-to-implement disaster recovery plan.
6. Accept nothing less than seamless integration for the bi-directional transfer of information between the EHR and PM components.

The final component—last, but certainly not least—is the billing component. How is the practice compensated for its services? Over the past decade or so, we've seen a transition from paper claim to electronic claim submission of charges. I won't go into the reason this has happened; suffice it to say however, that this was not necessarily to improve the delivery of healthcare or to improve physician reimbursements.

Traditionally, medical billing has been performed two primary ways: in-house and outsourced. In-house billing means that someone in the practice is required to enter the charges for each visit, submit the claims, and then follow up to see that the claims are paid. Outsourced billing means that the daily charges are sent to a vendor that has the responsibility to submit the claims and then follow up to see that the claims are paid. Many billing services find it difficult to justify a policy of indiscriminate follow-up for every underpayment or delay. This is due to the high cost of follow-up. When the difference between the cost of follow-up and the value of the insurance underpayment gets smaller, the incentive to leave the underpaid difference for the insurance company gets larger. The net result is that for many practices, large numbers of small underpayments are never collected. Even today, in the electronic realm, these two principal methods—in-house and outsourcing—remain; however, outsourcing can have significant advantages if the right service is used.

The biggest change in medical billing today is the introduction of technology designed to help track and follow up on claims. Most modern billing services offer a variety of reporting capabilities, providing the practice with a mechanism to measure the billing service's performance. Unfortunately, the ability of a typical billing service to effectively discover and follow up on underpayments is limited initially, and it deteriorates over time as payers find new tactics to impede and underpay claims. With the technological and financial resources available to the insurance companies, they've had the upper hand over the medical practitioner for many years. This is no longer an absolute. With economy of scale and the creation of a physician billing network, a sufficient volume of claims and payment data can be observed in a single aggregation platform database. This returns some leverage to the individual practices, and it helps restore balance between those practices and the insurance companies.

Consider these requirements when choosing a billing service:

1. Find a service with comprehensive monitoring of all underpayments and delays.
2. Look for disciplined follow-up on all underpayments and delays.
3. Ensure that your billing records are accessible 24/7/365.
4. Be certain that there's transparency and accountability at all levels, in real time.
5. Only consider a service with the ability to discover payer-specific underpayment patterns and claims processing rules, and the ability to implement appropriate updates to its database's claims processing logic in a timely fashion.

Now, imagine that you've begun to transition your practice into the 21st century by adding an EHR. You think you're sitting pretty, ready to take on the new government regulations and insurance industry standards. Congratulations. But what good is the EHR by itself if your office still uses paper and pen for the remainder of its work flow? Much of the information you'll work with will likely require redundant efforts either by you, your staff, or both. OK, so you realize that, in addition to EHR, you really need the PM component to improve efficiency in the office. Great! But what happens when you're done with your patient encounter and want to submit your charges? Oops, another stumbling block. To solve this problem, some PM/EHR vendors include software to help an in-house staff member submit and follow up on claims. This, however, does nothing to help the practice overcome the insurance companies' significant advantage. No matter how experienced the in-house staff member might be with billing, the fact remains that the practice stands alone against all of the insurance companies.

The ultimate solution is a fully integrated platform, seamlessly transferring data among the three components. The integrated platform should leverage the strength, skill, and experience of each component. Each practice knows best how to deliver its specific type of healthcare. They should also recognize the need to use proper tools, allowing them to focus on what they do best.

Vendors have spent millions, if not billions, of dollars researching and developing their various PM/EHR platforms. They should be the ones focusing on maintaining adherence to HIPAA, other government regulations, and various independent certifications. Since billing services can differ significantly with regard to their experience, performance, reliability, accountability, and compatibility with the PM/EHR platform components, it's essential that practices choose carefully. They should seek a vendor with a true physician network and a single aggregation platform database. Only with this type of technology in place can some semblance of parity be restored between the individual medical practice and the insurance companies.

Finally, in order for the integrated platform to provide relief to the practice when it comes to duplication/redundancy of work, there needs to be significant collaborative efforts between the PM/EHR platform and the billing service platform. With the future approaching fast and the handwriting on the wall, unless medical practices move toward totally integrated PM/EHR/billing system platforms, their economic future will be in doubt. Don't wait until it's too late. Be pro-active. Do your due diligence. Arm yourself now with the tools of the 21st century, or plan on going the way of the dinosaurs.

Consider these requirements when choosing a PM/EHR/billing service platform:

1. Ask if all components meet the requirements listed above.
2. Ask the PM/EHR vendor, "With which billing services are you integrated?"
3. Ask the billing service, "With which PM/EHR platforms are you integrated?"
4. Ask for references of both current and past clients.

About the Guest Author

Joseph Kamelgard, MD, FACS, worked his way through engineering school in a cooperative education program between Boston University and the National Aeronautics and Space Administration (NASA). He earned his medical degree at the Technion - Israel Institute of Technology in 1990. Kamelgard completed a residency in general surgery and two one-year fellowships (in cardiothoracic surgery and advanced laparoscopic surgery) as well as preceptorships and continuing education courses. He was appointed to the surgical faculty of the University of Medicine & Dentistry of New Jersey/New Jersey Medical School in 1998, where he remained for five years. Dr. Kamelgard left academia in 2003 to form Lighter for Life®, a surgical practice entirely devoted to the surgical treatment of morbid obesity. After five years in clinical practice, he formed Billing Integration Group (BIG). Its purpose is to develop fully integrated electronic platforms that combine practice management, electronic health records, and outsourced billing services.

Part VI

Outsourcing

If everybody minded their own business, the world would go around a great deal faster than it does.

—The Duchess
Alice's Adventures in Wonderland
Lewis Carroll

Outsourcing is one of the most promising growth directions for billing. This is due to opportunities for cross-continental labor arbitrage, limited resources within each individual medical practice, and centralized, Internet-based Vericle billing technology. Part VI starts with a discussion of cultural issues that are typical in any outsourcing decision, focusing on the cultural gap problem between the outsourcing and the outsourced organizations. Chapter 32 looks at the foreign exchange trends and their implications vis-à-vis global labor cost arbitrage as a major outsourcing decision component. Chapter 33 presents a "total cost of ownership" approach to outsourcing decision making. Chapter 34 analyzes the most frequent myths and facts about outsourced billing, including a close look at the notorious "zero-sum game" argument. Chapter 35 discusses SaaS (Software as a Service) in the limited context of outsourced software management, excluding the service component of the required solution. Chapter 36 concludes Part VI with a review of the outsourced lockbox selection method.

Chapter 31

An E-Myth Lesson in Cultural Gap Discovery

Dr. Ed Just woke up at two a.m. and was unable to fall asleep again. He went to his desk, logged onto his computer, and looked for the termination clause in his billing services agreement. He still had fresh memories of meeting the billing services president, who seemed both competent and pleasant to work with. She showed good references, had a great service attitude, and even agreed to reduce her price. As he recalled these promising signs, Dr. Ed then wondered why her collections were so low for the past six months? How was it possible that an accommodating service, which passed the most stringent scrutiny, failed to meet the simple billing needs of a small and seemingly easy-to-serve practice?

Typical risk-benefit analyses of whether or not to outsource medical billing invoke five kinds of argument: balance sheet, performance, control, focus, and zero-sum game. The debate then boils down to a checklist of a dozen steps for vendor selection. Nevertheless, it's often the case that billing services that have undergone close prior examination still don't meet the basic billing needs of a standard medical practice. The question then is this: what defines a reliable set of criteria for selecting a good medical billing service?

The answer seems to be far more related to the business culture differences between the practice and the service than to specific capabilities of the given service. Gerber's E-Myth theory applies well to both managing a medical practice and billing: a good doctor doesn't necessarily make a successful practice owner, and a good biller doesn't always develop a profitable and growing billing service.[96] In fact, most medical practices as well as billing services struggle, and often fail, because the founders are "technicians" who are inspired to start businesses, but they lack the business management skills and knowledge about how successful businesses run.

In Gerber's vernacular, doctors are "technicians" who are skilled at healing people, while billing "technicians" are skilled at billing and may enjoy coding. So, when "technicians" start their own billing operation, they continue doing the work they're skilled at—and, without access to solid technology and industrial-grade processes, they soon find themselves unable to scale up. Rather than working "on" the business, they work "in" the business. In other words, they simply own a job instead of a business. A scalable practice, just like a scalable billing service, requires disciplined performance measurement, process consistency, industrial-grade technology, and the discipline for systematic and continuous improvement.

If both the client (medical office) and vendor share the culture and the discipline for systematic and continuous improvement, then the billing service will be perceived as successful. A shared discipline will help pursue shared goals to build consistent and scalable services for patients and for medical practices. If, on the other hand, only one of the participants has a process to systematically scale up, while the other manages the practice or the service in an ad hoc manner, then a conflict is inevitable. Since the billing process involves humans (who err), and payers (who delay, underpay, and return for audits), then every

---

[96] Gerber, *E-Myth Revisited.*

billing service—even the best-organized ones—will face delays and underpayments.

The strength of a billing service must be tested in terms of its processes and technology to discover problems and improve the solutions. If the billing service has no such processes, it will fail. If the billing service has these processes, but the client practice has no appreciation or discipline to work together on establishing practice workflow processes, then the billing service will fail as well. Finally, if neither of the participants in the billing service relationship cares about consistency and scalability, then results are entirely unpredictable and potentially risky for both—in terms of not only lost revenue, but also potential fraud and compliance problems, audits, and associated penalties.

So, what's Dr. Ed to do next time he's in the market for a billing service? In-source? Outsource? These are not the right questions to ask. The right questions are: Do I want to build a scalable and consistent service for my patients? If so, what are the key components in my practice, and how do I make each one of them consistent and scalable?

Chapter 32

Outsourced Billing – Will It End in 2010?

India's dramatic economic growth has created some negative implications for offshore business process outsourcing organizations (BPOs). Some of these implications can be directly attributed to the devaluation of the U.S. dollar compared with the rupee. If this trend persists, and the U.S. dollar continues to lose its value against the rupee, only the most efficient BPOs in India will be able to continue making a profit.

Hundreds of healthcare practices and billing companies in the United States have outsourced their billing and transcription processing to India, taking advantage of the differences in economic development and favorable exchange rates. Outsourced billing processes typically include claims processing, coding, follow-up, and data entry of patient demographics as well as charge and payment data. Labor cost arbitrage between the United States and India has caused considerable heartache for numerous American transcription specialists, billers, and coders; many have had to find other jobs or learn new skills. But in the long run, the grand picture has paid off for both sides by creating new jobs in India, saving money in America, and creating more challenging and better-paying jobs for those who have stepped up to leadership and managerial roles in the new playing field.

The profits for both the outsourcing and the outsourced organizations depend directly on the exchange rate. If the rupee appreciates against the U.S. dollar, an Indian BPO suffers eroding profit margins. In the last six months of 2007, the rupee exchange rate dropped 12%, from 44–45 down to around 39 against the dollar.[97] Since American doctors are paid in U.S. dollars and not in rupees, the revenues of U.S. doctors or therapists, when translated to rupees, shrinks in step with the narrowing gap between the economic levels of these two countries and the melting exchange rate.

"For quite some time I've been reviewing the bottom line margin that started to dip considerably," writes Deepak P., head of the medical billing department in one of India's major business process outsourcing organizations. "During the past six months we adopted various methodologies to keep our cost down in all aspects (staff costs, technology, training, etc.) so as not to affect the billing rates with our clients. But with rupee exchange rate dropping to around 39 against USD and with no hope of depreciating over the next few quarters, we understand that it would be very difficult to sustain our margins going forward."[98]

Can a medical billing company with significant offshore labor components in India maintain its profit margins in 2008, against the background of the appreciating rupee? If not, should it reconsider the entire labor arbitration model and in-source at least some of the outsourced jobs?

If the U.S. dollar continues to lose its value against the rupee, it will become increasingly difficult for BPOs in India to be profitable. To afford the decreasing revenue per doctor, BPOs must be able to increase their volume of clients while simultaneously reducing their

[97] x-rates.com, *2007 – American Dollars to 1 INR*.

[98] Deepak P., personal communication, December 12, 2007.

workload for each client through automation and, perhaps, secondary outsourcing to other countries.

Chapter 33

Relative Value Price-Performance Calculation

Internet-based technology has been effectively applied to reduce medical billing costs, especially at the stages of electronic submission and scrubbing. However, excess focus on reducing the costs of individual process components, while ignoring total billing quality, exposes the medical practice to a significant financial downside. Quantification of billing quality, and its inclusion into the price-performance equation of billing service, yields a more comprehensive financial picture and better decisions about billing service selection and management. Such an approach also results in substantially higher remittance and better regulatory compliance. However, its effectiveness is subject to billing performance guarantees and transparency.

The traditional sequence of management steps to rationalize medical practice billing and reduce its costs requires the physician to invest in processes, personnel, and technology:

1. Study your denials to eliminate errors by using claims-scrubbing software.

2. Educate your front-end employees about the billing process, and know how to be a part of it.
3. Investigate tools for electronic submission, and take advantage of technology.
4. Set guidelines to determine which claims and which dollar amounts should be appealed.
5. Provide patients with clear payment policies up front.

ROI in Claims Processing Technology

For illustration, consider the case of a three-office practice with 17 internists and a panel of 20,000 patients. This is quite similar to Potomac Physician Associates in Bethesda, MD, which, in 2002, brought their claims submission and practice management services in-house.[99] Let's assume that three full-time equivalent persons (FTEs) work in billing and use an off-the-shelf electronic medical billing technology infrastructure, so annual costs are about $120,000 for personnel and $36,000 for technology. For reference, typical medical billing technology software performs claim validation, patient demographics and eligibility tests prior to a visit, electronic claim submission, comprehensive accounts receivable reporting, etc. (see Chapter 4). Additionally, by using this technology, 98% of claims are now clean, adding further value for the investment in claims processing technology. In this case, billing costs add up to $156,000 annually (Figure 17).

This is a significant accomplishment in terms of billing processing costs, because without advanced technology, the same practice may need at least seven FTEs at an annual cost of $280,000. Accordingly, the in-house billing services arrangement used before installing the new off-the-shelf technology cost at least $292,000 per year—$280,000 in FTEs plus an estimated $12,000 in a less expensive, albeit inferior, sys-

---

[99] Donato, "Three Steps to Fewer Denials."

tem. Thus, the $36,000 investment in superior technology saves at least $136,000 ($292,000 – $156,000) per year, which is obviously an impressive ROI.

Figure 17. The Effect of Technology on In-house Billing Costs

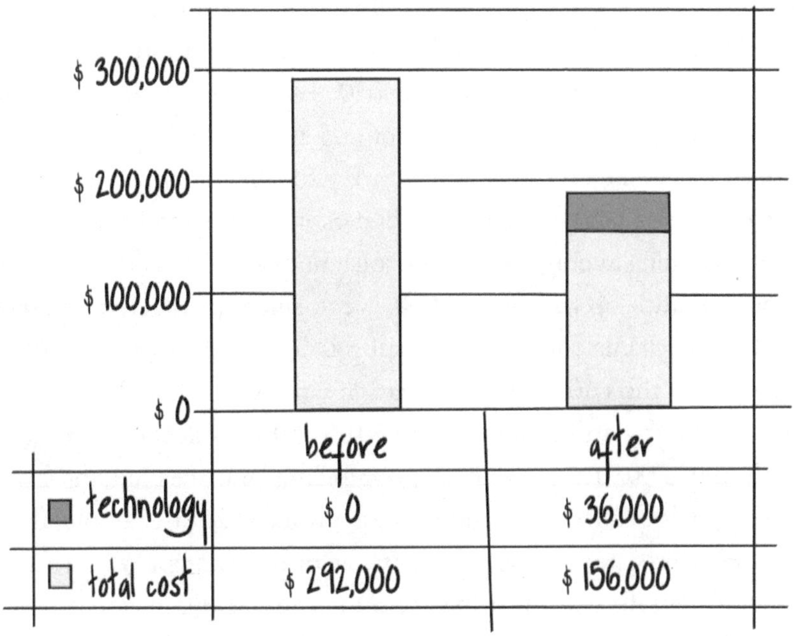

Investing in superior technology reduces overall in-house claims processing costs.

However, this approach does not account for the entire spectrum of costs associated with an in-house billing approach. It ignores the total revenue aspect of the billing function, which is its ultimate purpose.

Estimated Losses Due to Poor Billing Quality

To receive a more comprehensive perspective, let's compute the total losses generated by uncollected payments. We'll establish a convenient baseline and figure out a way to estimate the losses.

In our experience, the likelihood of payment shrinks dramatically with time. With a few exceptions, claims that are unpaid for more than four months are eventually forfeited—hence the importance of looking at accounts receivable beyond 120 days. Therefore, to compute total losses, we must start by computing total revenue, and then use the days in accounts receivable as a proxy for the underpayment.

For the case study at hand, we first estimate the total practice revenue by assuming average physician collections of $300,000; for 17 physicians, this adds up to a $5,100,000. Next, since the practice's percentage of clean claims for electronic submission is about average (98%), we'll also use the current average nationwide A/R beyond 120 days of about 17.7%[100]—so the losses on $5,100,000 in collections would approach $902,700. This is due to poor billing practices, coding errors, challenges with collections, and process problems. For example, the in-house biller may get to know patients, want to maintain good relationships, and therefore let overdue accounts slide. If the in-house biller is responsible for analyzing both accounts receivable and insurance company follow-up, she may decide to ignore certain accounts because she dislikes the follow-up tasks. Therefore, while the practice saves $136,000 on total costs upon installing an electronic claim scrubbing and submission infrastructure, it still loses an estimated $902,700 on billing quality. Total billing costs with the newly installed technology infrastructure are now $1,058,700—$902,700 (86%) in uncollected fees, $120,000 (11%) for personnel, and $36,000 (3%) for technology (see Figure 18).

---

[100] Lowes, "Practice Pointers."

Figure 18. Distribution of In-house Billing Costs and Uncollected Fees

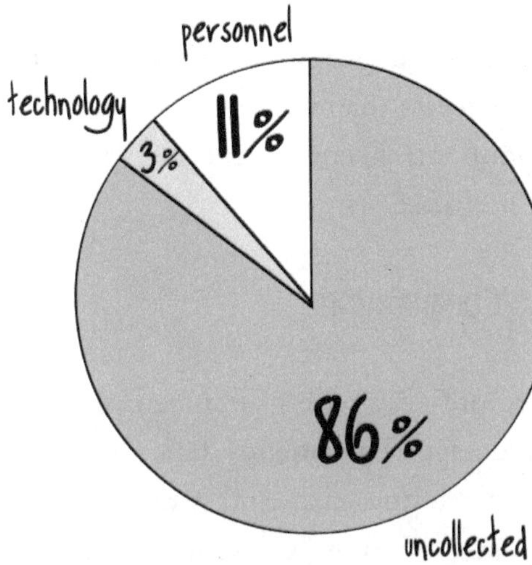

Improving collections quality yields significant benefits over any potential cost savings.

The lesson of this case study is that the billing function costs may be grossly underestimated because of the following common pitfalls:

- **Pitfall #1** – Focus on the costs of individual components of the billing function instead of computing the bottom-line cost to the practice.
- **Pitfall #2** – Underestimate the costs of these components (for personnel costs, these can be benefits, sickness, management, replacement, education, and vacations).
- **Pitfall #3** – Focus on the numbers or quality of claims instead of dollars billed and paid.

An alternative approach, oriented to the bottom line, guarantees improved revenue before spending a dime:

1. Measure your current percentage of A/R beyond 120 days, and assume (for the sake of conservative management) that the money is lost.
2. Find a billing service provider with significantly higher performance levels than your own solution.
3. Base your management decisions on total cost/performance metrics.

Price-Performance Computation

A billing service provider with guaranteed performance levels typically charges a percentage of payments. This approach aligns the interests of the biller and the physician, and it results in dramatically lower A/R beyond 120 days, often as low as 4% or even 2%. In our case study, the difference in remittance between the two approaches amounts to $463,020, or 9.08%, more to the bottom line (Figure 19).

Figure 19 compares in-house and outsourced billing arrangements for our earlier example. Here, the in-house billing costs (ignoring billing quality loss of $902,700) are $156,000, or about 3% of total collections of $5,100,000. In a typical in-house cost analysis, a low 3% fee compares favorably against outsourced billing service pricing, which is often anywhere between 6% and 10% (in our illustration, we use 8%). The comparison in Figure 19 makes two important points. First, billing quality has a major impact on total collections, often surpassing the service fee. Second, you must be careful to avoid comparing percentage fees in the abstract, without reference to the actual collection amounts and the effect of billing quality.

Note that billing quality is a key component of the billing cost computation, and the decision to outsource the billing service is based on a multifold improvement in billing quality. Such an improvement must be so great that only a billing provider specialist can create and

Figure 19. Bottom-line Comparison of In-house and Outsourced Billing

annual	current	outsourced
collections	$5,100,000	$5,473,050
quality loss A/R beyond 120 days	17.7%	4.0%
billing fees	3.0%	8.0%
added revenue		$526,050

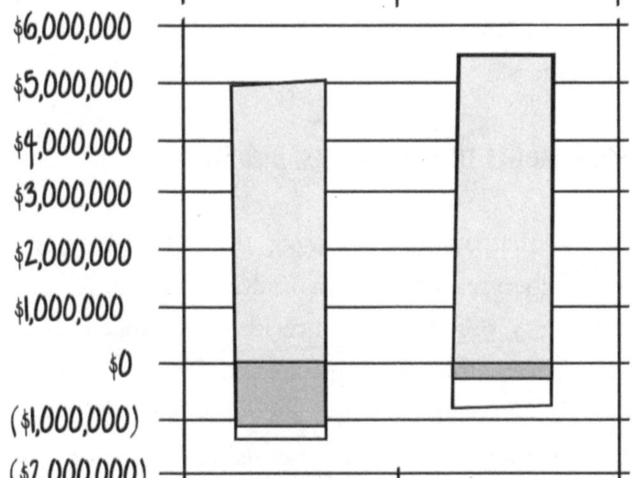

	current	outsourced
☐ revenue	$4,947,000	$5,473,050
☐ billing fees	($153,000)	($475,917)
☐ quality loss	($1,096,841)	($247,874)
costs	($1,249,841)	($723,791)

Improved billing quality with outsourcing yields better bottom line to the provider, despite higher billing fees.

maintain the required volumes and economies of scale. Therefore, consider outsourcing—or an alternative outsourced billing service provider—only after due diligence establishes that the billing provider delivers superior performance, the difference in performance is quantifiable and significant enough for bottom-line growth, and such performance can be verified independently and continuously. A rule of thumb is that the new combined percentage of fees and uncollected revenue must stay below in-house A/R (billing quality measured in terms of the percentage of the billed amount in A/R beyond 120 days). Note that the above analysis extends beyond comparing in-house and outsourced billing services; you can also use it to compare two outsourced billing service providers.

Additional Benefits of Outsourced Billing

Note also that by outsourcing to the right billing service provider, the practice liberates itself from multiple additional issues associated with the process, personnel, and technology aspects of billing. Specifically, the only remaining billing function for the practice owners is the periodic review of cash flow and accounts receivable—in other words, an entirely bottom-line-driven supervision. There's no need to micromanage the submission process, reconcile rejections, appeal to the payers, etc. Similarly, there's no more need to manage the billing employee team—their vacations, sick days, benefits, teamwork, and turnover. Finally, there's no longer a need to deal with any technology issues—such as installation, maintenance, backups, disaster recovery, HIPAA compliance, and upgrades.

Sensitivity Analysis

Previous analysis shows that total cost of billing depends on uncollected revenue. Therefore, billing method and vendor selection decision (in-house vs. outsourced) depend on the difference in remittance quality. A basic decision rule can be formulated as

> If $R_o + RF - R_oF < R_i - C_P - C_T$
> Then the practice should consider billing function outsourcing (Table 5)

Table 5. Billing Outsourcing Decision Rule	
Parameter	**Meaning**
R	Total billed revenue
R_o	Quality of the outsourced vendor, measured in terms of A/R beyond 120 days
R_i	Quality of the in-house function, measured in terms of A/R beyond 120 days
F	Outsourced fee
C_P	Cost of in-house personnel
C_T	Cost of in-house technology

Note that both the billing service providers and the practices can use this rule to establish the limit values to rationalize service as well as negotiate fees. For instance, if our case study's physician group improves in-house remittance quality so that A/R beyond 120 days drops from 17.7% to below 8.34%, then, subject to remaining constant parameters, the practice will do better by keeping the billing function in-house. On the other hand, if the provider's billing quality is at 17.7% or higher, then any fee below 17.7% is worth paying as long as the provider guarantees the A/R beyond 120 days below 4%. Finally, if the practice prefers to establish a fee limit, then the limit may be used to determine the required quality guarantee. For instance, if the provider agrees to pay 12%, then any A/R below 10% benefits the provider.

Pricing of Outsourced Billing Service

Given practice revenue, internal costs, and quality rates for in-house billing, we can now plot the values for optimal billing rate as a percentage of total revenues and a function of outsourced service quality. Assuming outsourced quality ranges between 2% and 18% and a constant in-house quality rate of 17%, 12%, and 8%, the optimal billing graph takes the form depicted in Figure 20.

Figure 20. Billing Quality and Service Pricing

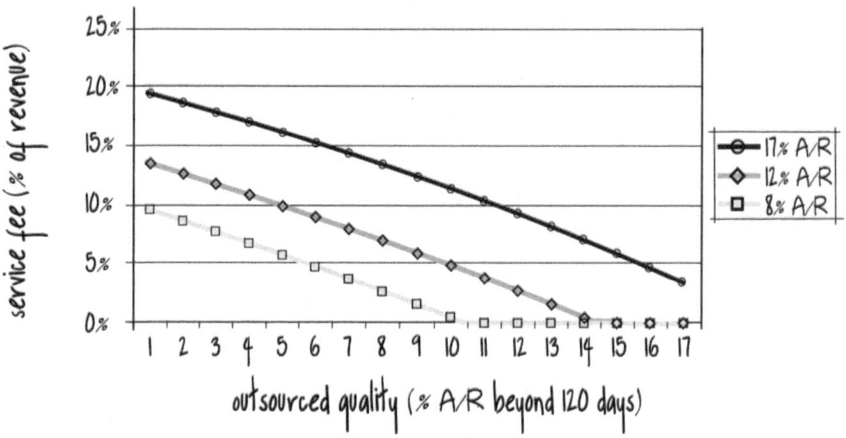

Outsourced billing quality rate family of 17%, 12%, and 8%.

Summary

We can draw three lessons about how to compute the cost of billing and select a better billing service provider:

1. **Costs** – Billing costs may be grossly underestimated because of neglect of uncollected revenue for
    a. In-house billing
    b. Outsourced billing

2. **Decision making**
    a. The financial difference between in-sourcing and

outsourcing may be huge, depending on the difference in respective performance.

  b. The billing service provider selection must be based, first of all, on billing quality.

3. **Selection** – Prior to hiring an outsourced service provider, make sure that the provider
   a. Guarantees billing quality
   b. Provides tools for continuous quality verification (transparency)

Chapter 34

Dilemma of Outsourced Billing Services

Statistics show that both in-house and outsourced billing services may deliver superior or inadequate billing performance. On one hand, only 5.66% of "better-performing practices" outsource their billing. In other words, the vast majority of "better-performing practices" achieve adequate billing performance in-house. On the other hand, less than 83% of payments are paid to an average practice within the first four months of the date of service. Worse, 59% of in-house billers do not review the explanations of benefits, and 55% of in-house billers have never appealed a denied claim. In other words, the average medical practice delivers almost one-fifth of its services for free because in-house billing fails to provide adequate payment performance.[101]

Can outsourced electronic medical billing software and service improve or expedite payments and reduce costs? This chapter revisits key arguments for and against outsourced billing in light of the increasing complexity and regulatory scrutiny of billing processes.

---

[101] Medical Association of Billers, *Salary and Statistics Survey*; Maguire, "Your Practice Claims Denied?"

Arguments FOR Outsourcing

1. Improved billing performance in spite of continuously reduced fee schedules, growing billing complexity, frequent audits, and payer consolidation into larger networks
2. Extra time to focus on patient care and/or practice development
3. Reduced operating costs

Billing performance improvement is typically measured in reduced accounts receivable, faster median payment, and reduced underpayment and denial ratios. The practice owner uses the extra time for family, patient care, or practice development. The cost gains are typically measured in the saved salaries and benefits of billing personnel who are no longer needed. It's important to keep in mind that a 10% improvement in overall billing quality means 10 times more to the practice's bottom line than a 1% reduction in billing fees. Therefore, if an outsourced billing service provider is able to significantly improve billing performance, the cost reduction may be marginal in comparison with a total contribution to the practice's bottom line.

Arguments AGAINST Outsourcing

1. Upcoding risk
2. Deficient follow-up

If the billing service charges a percentage of total collections, then, according to the upcoding argument, the service has an incentive to use a CPT code with a higher return, which often contradicts medical notes on hand. As the practice owner is ultimately responsible for the medical claims, such a billing service exposes the owner to upcoding felony charges. On the other hand, the practice owner with an in-house billing operation pays flat salaries to the billing personnel, eliminating the incentive for upcoding.

The deficient denial follow-up argument is a variation of a zero-sum argument. It's based on an assumption that a billing service provider's capacity for a follow-up process is limited and that clients must compete for it. A win for one client must necessarily be a loss for another. By driving such follow-up activity down to zero, the billing service provider wins at the expense of every one of its clients. The larger the client base of the billing service, the more it wins, while the payments to each individual client continue to shrink because of increasingly bad follow-up.

In the extreme case, when the electronic billing software and service provider has no ability to follow up at all (for instance, when the service is offered at excessively low prices, such as 4%), the provider ends up losing twice—first, by paying a fee for automatically paid claims, and then, by receiving no service on underpayments and leaving a major part of earned compensation to the insurer. On the other hand, the practice with an in-house billing operation has all of its billing capacity focused on follow-up for a single practice, so the in-house billing service will necessarily bring better results than the outsourced service.

Counter-Argument Analysis

- **Compliance** – The upcoding argument is irrelevant for doctors who code themselves by using an electronic, or even a paper, superbill. Next, if the biller is expected to code, then the practice owner must ensure that its compliance process protects both the practice and the billing service. The penalties for noncompliance have been steadily escalating in the last decade; today, those penalties include financial, licensure, and imprisonment aspects. A practice without a compliance process faces a higher risk of failing a random post-payment audit and paying higher penalties than a practice with a formal compliance process in place. Once a comprehensive process is implemented fully and reliably, the practice owner eliminates major risk, regardless of having the billing service in-house or outsourced.

- **Performance measurement** – Measuring billing quality exposes the fallacy of the "zero-sum game" argument. If a medical practice with in-house billing demonstrates a lower percentage of accounts receivable beyond 120 days than the national average of 17.7%,[102] then its billers do have better follow-up performance, and the analysis comes down to comparing total in-house costs with total billing office fees. Again, since a 10% improvement in overall billing quality means 10 times more to the practice's bottom line than a 1% reduction in billing fees, an outsourced billing service provider that charges a percentage of total collections has a larger incentive to improve overall payment performance than to sell the service to another medical practice.

Recent progress made by industry leaders, in terms of overall billing quality and included services, confirms this analysis. Aggressive up-front claim scrubbing, real-time compliance analysis, and automated denial follow-up are just a few activities provided by modern Vericle-type billing software to enable continuous improvement of billing performance in step with the growing scale and number of clients. Other important developments are billing workflow integration with practice management tools—including patient scheduling, electronic medical records (EMR) or SOAP notes—and real-time reporting and alert generation.

---

[102] Lowes, "Practice Pointers."

Summary

In conclusion, abstract arguments for and against outsourced electronic medical billing are pointless, because both sides can be shown as right or wrong, depending on specific and quantitative performance measures. Practice owners must establish objective performance and compliance criteria, and they must use them systematically and within the individual practice's context when addressing the question of outsourced medical billing.

Chapter 35

Nine Criteria for Best SaaS

Software as a Service (SaaS) pushes the limits of outsourcing and reduces the exorbitant costs of specialized practice management software. An SaaS model is available for all aspects of medical practice management—including scheduling, billing, and SOAP note documentation, which are mission-critical for high-quality healthcare, practice building, and regulatory compliance.

What Is Software as a Service?

Software as a Service (SaaS) is a logical step in the progression from build to buy to subscribe, and it's a manifestation of a major software trend toward service-oriented architecture (SOA). SaaS is the software industry term for delivery of software products and services over a network (typically the Internet) under a subscription business model.

The increasing reliability of the Internet, coupled with the availability of completely integrated practice management and billing software, creates supportive conditions for the "pay as you go" business model. SaaS liberates the users in two significant ways:

1. SaaS requires no large up-front investment in hardware and software licenses on the part of the user.

2. SaaS shifts the onus of systems management from the user to the SaaS vendor, including the following:
    a. Internet connectivity, bandwidth, and routers
    b. Servers for web server software, email, and firewalls
    c. Capacity management
    d. Redundancy management
    e. Application upgrade management

In financial management terms, the SaaS proposition is equivalent to turning capital expense into operating expense, which translates into the following:

1. Better balance sheets
2. Lower risk, especially during the period of rapid technology innovation on one hand and practice-building stages on the other hand

SaaS differs from application service providers (ASPs) in two ways: domain expertise and software development skills. While ASP vendors have developed primarily hardware and systems expertise and offered foreign business applications, SaaS vendors are experts in the specific application domain.

SaaS Vendor Selection

For the medical practice manager, the main challenge could be integrating newer applications with the subscribed SaaS application. SaaS integration platforms (SIPs) are a popular way to handle the integration challenge. An SIP, such as Vericle, offers a suite of integrated applications, including patient relationship management, patient scheduling, SOAP notes, and billing.

A medical practice in search of an SaaS vendor must focus on the following factors:

1. **Functionality** – Does the application deliver the required functionality?
2. **Training** – Will the vendor provide sufficient application training?
3. **Third-party application interface** – Does the application work with other applications already deployed in the office? What requirements must be satisfied if you decide to purchase another application later?
4. **Performance** – How do you measure application performance? Are formal performance metrics available continuously?
5. **HIPAA compliance** – What controls are in place to enable access on a "need to see" basis only? Is every access instance logged using a secure mechanism?
6. **Service level agreement (SLA)** – What minimum service levels does the vendor guarantee to the client? What are the penalties for violating the SLA?
7. **Data ownership** – Who owns the data?
8. **Disaster recovery** – How long would it take to recover from a disaster? Is a secondary data center available 24/7?
9. **Disengagement procedures** – How long is data available upon severing the relationship? Who is responsible for data transfer to the new vendor?

Chapter 36

Lockbox Selection Process

A lockbox helps a medical practice streamline HIPAA-compliant mail processing and same-day check deposits. Electronic access to scanned documents, including EOBs, simplifies key office and billing processes and achieves multiple benefits:

- **Reliability** – Better revenue-cycle reliability via eliminating dependency on staff or on the billing service to handle checks.
- **Transparency** – Allows bi-directional verification of check deposits between the bank and the billing service. The doctor can personally verify deposits 24/7 via a secure Internet connection. There are no lost checks.
- **Billing efficiency** – Faster and better-controlled submission of secondary claims.
- **Patient service efficiency** – Simpler and faster resolution of patient account inquiries and disputes.
- **Added interest revenue** – Automated or semi-automated posting of insurance and patient payments. Checks are deposited upon arrival. Deposits are automatically invested

(via automatic sweep) in a money market account that earns interest. The doctor's money is never idle.

Lockbox Operation

Practice mail arrives directly to the lockbox, which provides the following service:

- All mail is opened and archived in a document management system, including scanning and indexing for future retrieval.
- Images are available to the practice or billing service via a secure, encrypted website.
- All checks received that day are deposited.
- Practice administrative staff has direct access to web-driven interfaces for mail, check queries, and reports.

Lockbox Implementation

A lockbox service is typically offered by two kinds of providers:

1. Large-scale, Vericle-like billing service vendor as part of service
2. Specialized financial institution (e.g., bank)

Lockbox Selection

Use the following criteria to choose a lockbox service:

1. **HIPAA compliance** – Can the service guarantee access only on a "need to know" basis and only to qualified staff? Are all required privacy and security measures in place? Is

there a solid disaster recovery capability and process?

2. **Quality assurance process** – What measures are taken to ensure timely error identification, correction, and tracking? Is there sufficient QA (quality assurance) process transparency to allow the practice owner complete control of mail and checks?

3. **Intuitive user interface** – How many steps are required to find a letter, EOB, or check? What are mail and check indexing parameters?

4. **Batch interfaces** – Is there a convenient way to download all or partial content of the document management system for upload to other systems (such as a billing system) or to an alternative lockbox provider facility?

5. **Time frames** – How long does it take to open mail, scan it into a document management system, and deposit a check? What is the time horizon for archived image storage? What is the time period for storage of original paper before shredding?

Lockbox Complexities

Consider the following additional issues:

1. The lockbox must be fully implemented. A partial implementation only increases management complexity.
2. The lockbox adds a headache for payers. All payers need to change your mailing address, which adds the likelihood of errors during the transition period.

Summary

Lockbox services lower administrative costs, increase staff productivity, and close collection cycles faster. A more efficiently run practice and happier staff mean more satisfied patients.

Chapter 37

Medical Billing Transformation – Change Leadership

Practice owners seeking better solutions often start with a vision of increased practice profitability while treating reasonable patient volumes. Their vision spans multiple aspects, including better reach to prospective patients, better reimbursement rates, full and timely payments by insurance companies, less time spent on visit documentation, improved documentation quality for better clinical follow-up and lower audit risk, and more free time for family. However, that vision conflicts directly with the payers' goals to reduce costs and increase revenues. Payers' goals are in direct conflict with a provider's vision, because cost savings for payers simply mean that providers treat more patients at lower reimbursement rates—or, in other words, providers work harder for less money.

In addition to the basic payer-provider conflict, visionary practice owners must also face the resistance of their own office managers and colleagues. These people may be skeptical because they don't trust the owner, or because they've seen five other initiatives that all failed, or they think they might lose something with the change. Significant time, enthusiasm, and resources are needed to change practice processes and technology and to retrain personnel, while at the same time managing the practice and treating patients. The challenge of overcoming resistance to change and implementing it in your practice is akin to enhancing airplane engineering while keeping the plane in the air. Thus, medical practice owners often find themselves on the horns of a dilemma between adopting the new solutions or compromising the vision and returning to the old ways, along with shrinking revenues and growing frustration.

John Kotter, a Harvard Business School professor and the world's foremost authority on leadership and change, discovered that transformation challenges span across multiple industries and share the same characteristics. His book *Leading Change* lists an eight-step process for implementing successful transformations. To improve the odds of solving change management problems and reducing failure risk, it's useful to prepare for five classes of change challenges: complacency, limited sharing of the vision, different obstacles to the vision, inability to accomplish short-term wins, and failure to solidify the change in the practice culture.

Let's look at each of these challenges:

1. **Complacency** – This is the most deadly of practice change management problems. If you just plunge ahead with a new electronic medical records (EMR) system or billing process, without first establishing a shared sense of immediate need or urgency because of increased audit risk or shrinking revenue, then natural complacency takes over—and the entire change effort fails. It's hard to drive people out of their comfort zones. Past failures, the lack of a visible crisis, low performance standards, and insufficient feedback from doctors, office personnel, and patients—these all add up to turning the best-intended change initiatives into talk with-

out substance.

2. **Limited sharing of the vision** – Don't underestimate the need for, and power of, a shared vision. Running a practice is a complex balancing act between multiple priorities, competing demands for shared resources, and crisis management. Vision is required to align the multiple, and often conflicting, initiatives toward the common goal and to maintain the right priorities. Without a clearly articulated vision of better payments, reduced workload, improved practice workflow, and better billing process control, the decision-making process drowns in endless details and unresolved conflicts.

3. **Different obstacles to the vision** – Smart and well-intentioned managers and practice owners often avoid confronting roadblocks created by misaligned personal incentives or wrong organizational structures. They end up disempowering employees and undermining the entire change process. If better payments are part of your vision, then you can't allow your billing manager to get away with excuses for growing accounts receivable, undisciplined follow-up with your office staff or insurance companies, or ineffective appeal letters.

4. **Inability to accomplish short-term wins** – Without short-term wins, it's hard to keep the team motivated. For instance, if better patient visit compliance is part of your vision, and you plan to implement it using technology for automated patient reminder calls, then you must count your no-shows every day and demonstrate both reduced no-shows and increased revenue that's directly attributable

to the shrinking no-shows.

5. **Failure to solidify the change in the practice culture** – The new organization structure, the new processes, and the new technology platform used to implement the change—every practice component must be based on the changed reality. Otherwise, the old habits return and the benefits disappear, thus shrinking practice revenues and increasing workload for not only the office manager but also the providers.

The pain of not optimizing practice management manifests itself in the extra time required to do medical procedures—while worrying about upcoding fraud, the extra time it takes to meet charting requirements, the extra effort required to bill and collect payments, the time it takes to meet patient notification requirements, and the need to face patients who demand more time for questions. It all adds up to longer work hours, lower job satisfaction, lower reimbursements, and added frustration.

The provider's choices boil down to implementing changes now or waiting for solutions that help manage the payer-provider conflict, yet allow for easier implementation, minimizing the resistance to change.

Today's Internet offers an alternative choice, which is based on the simple idea of aggregating claim volumes and the technology resources needed to manage them. Networked Internet technology is, at last, mature enough to enable massive claim aggregation and processing—from traditional claim "scrubbing," to payer submissions, to payment reconciliations, to automated comparisons with contractually allowed amounts, to various workflow models—and it's available now for small practices and billing offices. By capitalizing on networked Internet technology, a growing number of practice owners have implemented their visions of systemic practice improvements. These practice owners create a "network effect" by consolidating and sharing practice management and billing processes, technology, and human resources.

Why let your competitors take advantage of such networked solutions ahead of you?

Part VII

Billing Performance Indexing

It's a poor sort of memory that only works backward.

—The Queen
Through the Looking Glass
Lewis Carroll

The first step in developing any methodology is performance evaluation and standardization of performance benchmarking methods. Part VII documents the first attempt to develop a rigorous medical billing methodology, which allows a systematic and repeatable evaluation of both the billing office performance and the payer payment performance. Chapter 38 starts the benchmarking discussion by looking at a Wall Street indexing technique and selecting a rule-based benchmarking proxy. Chapter 39 applies the earlier concepts to evaluate both billers and payers. The final chapter in Part VII demonstrates the process of constructing a frequency-based annual index.

Chapter 38

A Context-driven, Rule-based Approach to Relative Benchmarking

The first step in developing any methodology is performance evaluation and standardization of performance benchmarking methods. The payment performance index is a benchmarking technique inspired by prominent Wall Street firms that have little tolerance for walking away from money. When evaluating trader performance, Wall Street uses the context of the entire market to give a more accurate picture. The profit or loss for a given company may or may not mean success or failure of that company's market-traded securities, depending on the direction and movement of the markets in which those instruments trade. It's all about context, because in financial trading, markets are every bit as influential as profits on stock price in the short term.

Most large sell-side brokerage firms on Wall Street compute various indices on a daily basis. By comparing the performance of a trader's investment portfolio with that of an entire index, one can immediately determine if the trader has been successful or is failing relative to the entire market; this can be more meaningful than absolute numbers for a given security or portfolio.

The most popular indexing technique on Wall Street is rule-based; pre-defined rules select the instruments to include in an index, depending on specific parameter values of those instruments at the time of computation. The advantage of rule-driven indexing is that participation is dynamically determined at a point in time, reflecting the dynamic nature of the entire market. Today's top-10 list of index performers may not include the same names next week. A financial instrument's specific performance is recomputed every time the index itself is computed, reflecting the dynamic nature of performance relative to the market itself. If an instrument performs well in a strong market, the index takes this into account, since most participants are also doing well. The same is true on the downside—if a financial instrument performs poorly in a down market, the index clarifies that this may not be because of some inherent weakness in the company itself; rather, performance is reflected in the context of the entire market environment in which that security trades.

As an example, Lehman Brothers publishes its famous Fixed Income Index using a rule-based computing process that includes both basic characteristics (e.g., trade volume) and advanced risk parameters (e.g., duration and convexity).[103] By comparing the performance of a trader's investment portfolio with that of an entire index, you can immediately determine whether or not a trader has been successful relative to the entire market.

A similar indexing approach promises to redefine the payer-provider standoff in healthcare as well. A payer might be considered for inclusion in an index if total processed volume in the past month

---

[103] On September 22, 2008, Barclays Capital completed its acquisition of Lehman Brothers' North American investment banking and capital markets businesses. As part of the transaction, Lehman Brothers indices have become part of Barclays Capital. Recognizing the industry significance of these indices, Barclays is committed to maintaining the family of Lehman Brothers indices and the associated index calculation, publication, and analytical infrastructure and tools, including Lehman Brothers' POINT system.

exceeded a certain amount (say, $100 million). Participation in the index would be driven by multiple criteria, starting with a necessary minimum threshold of submitted claims, and including the all-important billing performance index. Payer participation in the index is defined dynamically at the time of computation, not by a static listing of specific payers. Therefore, any specific payer may or may not be included in the index for a given month, depending on that payer's performance.

For example, in June 2007, the Billing Performance Index (BPI)[104] stood at 14.8,[105] almost 3% below the national average of 17.7% (a BPI of 14.8 means that the average of the 10 top-performing payers that work with Billing Precision clients have 14.8% of accounts receivable beyond 120 days). BPI is a key billing performance characteristic because it's an indicator of claims that are never paid. Obviously, the lower the index, the better the billing performance. But this statistic is meaningful only when considered in the context of the relative performance of other payers.

Let's look at a comparative example. The December 2007 BPI improved 0.8% from its November mark, reaching 18.8—but this was still 6.2% worse than the national average of 17.7.[106] The December index, just like the November and October indices, maintained both its membership (the same top-performing payers) and the two lead positions: Medicare Illinois and Blue Cross and Blue Shield of Illinois. Table 6 details the November and December 2007 indexes as recorded by Billing Precision.

In summary, simply comparing a payer's performance metric with a national benchmark determines if that payer performs well. This approach to benchmarking also allows ranking within an entire set of

---

[104] BPI is developed and produced monthly by Billing Precision, LLC, an outsourced billing service provider that specializes in chiropractic billing using Vericle's technology.

[105] Lirov, "Chiropractic Office Billing Software."

[106] Lirov, "Chiropractic Office Billing Index."

Table 6. Monthly Billing Performance Index – December vs. November 2007			
	Payer	**Dec. BPI**	**Nov. BPI**
1	Medicare Illinois (same rank)	6.8	5.8
2	Blue Cross and Blue Shield of Illinois (same rank)	8.1	7.9
3	CIGNA (improved rank from #4)	10.7	15.7
4	Horizon Blue Cross Blue Shield of New Jersey (improved rank from #7)	13.9	20.7
5	Aetna (improved rank from #6)	14.8	20.0
6	Medicare New Jersey (lost rank from #5)	18.8	19.4
7	UnitedHealthcare (lost rank from #3)	21.2	15.0
8	GEICO (improved rank from #9)	35.2	36.2
9	Blue Cross Blue Shield of Georgia (improved rank from #10)	43.3	39.9
10	Blue Cross Blue Shield Pennsylvania (lost rank from #8)	43.4	30.5
	Average of 10 top-performing payers	18.8	19.6

Source: Billing Precision.

payers; you can sort them according to the same performance metric. And benchmarking allows you to identify elite payers—those that perform best compared with every payer in the country, as shown by the index-driven ranking. Finally, since the billing index represents the performance of an entire set of participants, the number of times a given payer has been selected determines its historic performance. UnitedHealthcare, for example, led chiropractic billing performance in 2006; it was included in Billing Performance Index seven times, maintaining a BPI value between 5 and 12.

Chapter 39

Billing Quality – Comparative Analysis Using Performance Index

It's good to have choices. And if you're a provider staring at a list of accounts receivable that are creeping up on 120 days, those choices become meaningful. The way to choose is by using the power of indexing to compare payment performance among insurance companies on a level playing field that ranks payers according to selected criteria.

The same indexing concepts that quantify and rank payers can also be used to rank medical billing services. There are two limitations to consider:

1. **Scope** – Since each medical billing service submits claims only to a defined subset of payers—those that insure the patients of the providers served by that billing service—the scope of an individual billing service index is limited by those claims. For example, if a service works with only three payers, its index has an entirely different scope than that of a service that works with 12 payers; one bad apple in a field of three can skew the whole picture.

2. **Perspective** – Scope isn't the only variable in understanding indexing. The perspective of the billing service is also important. Since each of the providers served by a biller sees only a subset of the total patient population insured by a given payer, the provider's perspective is limited by the number of patients that the provider sees. Data obtained from 19 patients is more easily skewed by aberrations than data from a patient base of 3,000.

These indexing limitations, scope and perspective, drive the distinction between "ideal" and "partial" payer performance indices. An "ideal" medical billing performance index is computed from comprehensive statistics across all providers nationally, irrespective of the billing service that helped process the claims. A "partial" payer's performance index is computed from statistics across all providers who are served by a specific billing service or individual provider. So, using the "ideal" index, healthcare providers can see which payers perform best across the board, and by using a "partial" index, providers can ascertain how a payer is doing with a specific billing service's claims.

In other words, the rule of thumb is to know your index to understand your payer. Obviously, index quality is directly proportional to scope and perspective: the wider the scope and the broader the perspective of the billing service associated with an index, the better the resulting data. While the "partial" performance index, computed on the basis of a specific biller's observations, only approximates the "ideal" index, it's the only realistic payer performance index available today. Since medical billing services use different billing processes and technologies, such partial indices rank the same payers differently—and, in fact, they may contain different payer members at different points during the same month. In this sense, the "partial" medical billing index becomes a characteristic of the billing service, instead of the payer; this allows providers to select the best medical billing service available based on this data, and it challenges billers across the nation to continuously improve their service quality.

How to Compute Your Medical Billing Index

At first glance, navigating the landscape of statistical payer and billing service indices may seem about as simple as rewiring your phone system. But it's not as difficult as it seems—all you need is a calculator and the following procedure:

- **Step 1** – Compute the percentage of your receivables that have aged beyond 120 days for each individual payer (insurance company) to whom you submit claims.
- **Step 2** – Weight-average them across all your payers. This emphasizes the payers to whom you submit the most claims versus lesser-used insurers.
- **Step 3** – Compare your payer index results with the monthly Billing Performance Index, which is available online.[107]
- **Step 4** – If your index is higher, then your office billing process might benefit from improvements.

[107] Lirov, "Chiropractic Billing Performance Index."

Chapter 40

Annual Billing Performance Index Summary – 2007

Billing Precision's annual Billing Performance Index (BPI) reflects payer performance stability over time based on chiropractic CPT codes. In 2007, BPI changed in several ways: Blue Cross and Blue Shield of Illinois (BCBS IL) took over the first position from UnitedHealthcare; BCBS IL was included in every monthly BPI during 2007. Its performance is especially impressive compared with the seventh place it held in 2006.

The monthly BPI lists the 10 best-paying insurance companies in that month, selected according to multiple criteria—e.g., minimal processed claim volume. In contrast, the annual BPI simply counts the frequency of the payer's participation in the monthly BPI for that year. A low percentage of accounts receivable beyond 120 days is critical to being included in the billing index. However, the frequency of inclusion in the index is a more robust performance metric, because it also measures billing performance consistency over a longer time period.

Table 7 lists the insurance companies that made the BPI 2007 listing, along with their average, low, and high billing index for the year.

No. of Months Included	Rank/Payer	BPI Avg.	BPI Low	BPI High
Table 7. 2007 Annual Billing Performance Index				
12	1. Blue Cross and Blue Shield of Illinois	10.9	7.1	16.0
11	2. CIGNA	13.4	8.9	24.1
	3. Medicare New Jersey	15.7	7.5	20.5
10	4. Aetna	16.6	8.8	22.1
	5. UnitedHealthcare	17.2	11.3	23.2
7	6. Medicare Illinois	14.0	5.8	30.4
	7. Horizon Blue Cross Blue Shield of New Jersey	18.0	13.9	24.3
	8. Blue Cross Blue Shield Pennsylvania	23.5	12.4	43.4
5	9. Blue Cross Blue Shield of Georgia	34.1	22.9	43.3
4	10. Blue Cross and Blue Shield of South Carolina	19.1	12.4	34.1
3	11. Blue Cross Blue Shield of Michigan	6.8	3.2	13.6
	12. Blue Cross and Blue Shield of Texas	15.2	10.3	20.0
	13. GEICO	34.9	33.4	36.2
2	14. Anthem Blue Cross and Blue Shield (Colorado)	9.6	6.8	12.3
	15. Humana	9.9	7.9	11.8
	16. Medicare Wisconsin	29.4	29.1	29.7
1	17. PHCS	0.3		
	18. QualCare	0.9		
	19. Atlantic Administrators	1.2		
	20. Unicare	9.6		
	21. Principal Life Insurance	10.6		
	22. GHI	11.5		
	23. CBSA	12.4		
	24. Medicaid Pennsylvania	5.1		
	25. Assurant	15.4		
	26. Blue Cross and Blue Shield of Alabama	21.3		
	27. Great West	22.0		
	28. Medicare Pennsylvania	23.1		
	29. Medicaid Illinois	36.7		

Source: Yuval Lirov (2008). "Chiropractic Billing Performance Index 2007 – Ten Best-Paying Insurance Companies."

Part VIII

Patient Relationship Management

"But I don't want to go among mad people," Alice remarked.

"Oh, you can't help that," said the Cat. "We're all mad here. I'm mad. You're mad."

"How do you know I'm mad?" said Alice.

"You must be," said the Cat, "or you wouldn't have come here."

—*Alice's Adventures in Wonderland*
Lewis Carroll

The key value proposition of patient relationship management, or PRM (also known as customer relationship management, or CRM, outside of healthcare), is its ability to enhance financial performance of the clinic by helping retain current patients and attract new patients. PRM helps provide timely, patient-centered, and efficient care, emphasizing preventive instead of reactive care. PRM is a data-driven and patient-focused methodology for strategic practice building and effective patient relationship development.

PRM helps identify new service needs, and then helps design care programs and processes for front office and billing functions to meet those needs. A PRM system captures patient information during the entire period of each care plan in terms of functional health improvement, care plan implementation, and billing.

Chapter 41 discusses profitability and the impact of office workflow on patient loyalty. Chapter 42 focuses on provider-patient email communication. Several advanced techniques for patient scheduling and appointment reminders are reviewed in Chapters 43 and 44.

Chapter 41

Patient Loyalty and Profitability

Patient loyalty is a key to continued practice success in terms of both recurring and new revenue. As patients keep returning to your practice, you maintain revenue stability—and as patients refer their friends and families, your practice billing collections grow. In terms of profitability, new patient acquisition is, by an order of magnitude, more expensive than loyalty maintenance for existing patients.

Time delay is a major problem of eroding patient loyalty. By the time you discover that you have a patient loyalty problem, it's typically too late to do anything about the patients who have already left. Patients typically desert you without saying good-bye, and your only way to discover patient attrition is by observing lower collections and more free time on your appointment scheduler.

Frequent patient communication is the only effective way to reduce such a time delay and increase the likelihood of timely loyalty problem identification and resolution. Such patient communications can revolve around any of the practice management components—from patient scheduling to SOAP notes to special healthcare literature to medical billing, insurance payments, co-pays, and deductibles.

Patient Identification for Targeted Communications

It's convenient to view targeted communications from the patient visit perspective:

- Patients due for scheduled appointments or who owe you payments need a reminder.
- Patients who recently had an appointment need results, interpretation, prescriptions, and follow-up.
- Patients with prescriptions that are about to expire may need to schedule a visit.
- Patients who have not had an appointment for a long time need a reminder to schedule a checkup. A screening procedure schedule should be generated using specific combinations of procedure (CPT) and diagnosis (ICD) codes.
- Patients with chronic conditions or permanent injuries need literature about recent progress in treating their conditions.
- Patients who have had a long series of appointments need progress reports.
- Patients who receive good progress reports need to be solicited for referrals.
- Patients with bad progress reports need special literature and special appointments.
- Patients waiting in the reception area need access to customized information about their specific conditions.

To generate such lists of patients, your systems must combine scheduling, medical notes, and billing data in a single database.

Patient Communications Venue

While traditional phone and conventional mail systems are still in use, the Internet is the most obvious choice for communicating with patients. A custom, HIPAA-compliant patient portal is the least expensive way to allow your patients to interact with you outside the clinic at their convenience and privacy. Patients can do the following:

- Review reminders and schedule appointments
- Review visit results
- Ask you clarifying questions
- Request prescriptions
- Read special literature and progress reports that you send them
- Send you referrals
- Review medical bills and pay invoices
- Track their medical costs

Active patient loyalty management, based on selective patient identification for targeted communications at the patient's convenience, is one of the most effective ways to improve practice profitability.

Chapter 42

Email for Billing and Personal Health Communications Between Physicians and Patients

Dr. Ed looked at the computer screen and thought about how to best respond to Pat, one of his patients. Dr. Ed was worried about the growing number of email messages arriving from his patients. Pat kept sending him at least two emails a day; some were about mundane billing issues, and some had fairly involved questions about her health. If Dr. Ed responded to every one of his patients' emails, he might soon find himself spending more time in front of the computer screen than seeing live patients. He liked email's immediacy and increased frequency of interaction with his patients, but he was also worried about HIPAA: what if his response got into the wrong hands? Would he be liable for breaking privacy laws?

Although over 85% of physicians have high-speed Internet access, physician-patient email is only now beginning to traverse the uphill slope of the adoption curve.[108] A recent study of 4,203 physicians,

[108] Brooks and Menachemi, "Physicians' Use of Email."

practicing in ambulatory settings, showed only modest advances in adopting email communication, and little adherence to recognized guidelines for email correspondence. While 63% indicated using email to correspond with nonpatients, only 16.6% had personally used email to communicate with patients, and only 2.9% frequently used email with patients.[109]

While physicians seem to adopt email communication in every aspect of clinic management, such as patient registration and insurance billing, several financial and legal issues impede physicians from regularly using email to communicate with patients. For instance, responding to patient email messages represents an "opportunity cost" to some physicians, especially if the email doesn't replace other modes of communication, such as telephone messages and traditional letters.

The aforementioned study indicated that email use correlated with the following:

- Age (use decreased with physicians over 61)
- Race (use decreased with physicians of Asian background)
- Medical training (use increased with family medicine or surgical specialties)
- Practice size (use varied with practices under or over 50 physicians)
- Geographic location (use in urban practices was 17.2%, while use in rural practices was only 7.9%)[110]

Remarkably, in this study, only 46 physicians (6.7%) adhered to at least half of the 13 selected guidelines for email communication:

1. Print email communications and place in patients' charts.

---

[109] Ibid.
[110] Ibid.

2. Inform patients about privacy issues with respect to email.
3. When email messages become too lengthy, notify patients to phone or come in to discuss the issue.
4. Establish a turnaround time for messages.
5. Ask patients to put their names or identification numbers in the body of the email message.
6. Send a new message to inform the patient that a request was completed.
7. Establish types of transactions (e.g., separate billing from clinical issues).
8. Explain to patients that their messages should be concise.
9. Remind patients when they don't adhere to guidelines.
10. Develop archival and retrieval mechanisms.
11. Include the category of transaction (e.g., billing) in the email's subject line.
12. Configure an automatic reply to acknowledge receipt of patients' messages.
13. Ask patients to use auto-reply features to acknowledge a clinician's message.[111]

In summary, both patients and doctors demonstrate increased use of Internet and email communication with each other for both administrative (e.g., billing) and personal health issues, but few physicians adhere to recommended email communication guidelines.

[111] Brooks and Menachemi, "Physicians' Use of Email."

Chapter 43

No-Show Risk Management

Most clinics lose an average of 20% of their revenue due to missed appointments.[112] Lost revenue may not be the largest problem caused by no-shows. Other problems span health damage, patient liability risks, reduced accessibility, and impeded resident education. Rigorous no-show management methods using powerful Vericle-like technologies, which integrate scheduling and billing data, reduce no-show rates and improve associated revenues by more than 50%.

No-Show Frequency Distribution

No-show rates average about 20%: 10% of clinics have less than 10% no-shows, 42% of clinics have 10%–20%, 34% of clinics have 20%–30%, and 14% of clinics have more than 30% no-shows. Further, the top 10 clinics in terms of lowest no-show rates range from 3%–9% for no-shows, while the bottom 10 clinics reach 33%–57%.[113]

---

[112] Hashim, Franks, and Fiscella, "Effectiveness of Telephone Reminders."

[113] Moore, Wilson-Witherspoon, and Probst, "Time and Money."

No-Show Impact to Clinic

A missed appointment poses five kinds of problems:

1. **Health damage** – A patient's health can be damaged due to interrupted continuity of care or a missed opportunity to solve an acute health problem. The doctor also loses an opportunity for a timely review of patient health, treatment progress, etc.

2. **Liability risk** – A patient who misses an appointment and suffers an injury may have a viable cause for a lawsuit against the practice. To avoid such risk, the doctor must maintain evidence of giving clear directions and making reasonable efforts to ensure the patient's compliance with the care program, including keeping follow-up appointments.

3. **Reduced accessibility** – Other patients are postponed and don't get access to care because of a no-show or canceled appointment.

4. **Impedance to medical education** – A resident or intern misses an opportunity to learn and improve care skills.

5. **Loss of revenue** – The clinic is unable to make up revenue due to missed appointments.

Three-Phase No-Show Management Strategy

An effective no-show management strategy is based on tracking, rescheduling, and follow-up:

1. **Tracking**
    a. Record all no-shows, and reconcile them with billing on a daily basis.
    b. Record no-show reasons and follow-up notes in patient records.
    c. Review end-of-day reports daily.

2. **Rescheduling in real time**
    a. Allow patients to request appointments online using the Internet.
    b. Overbook, and use waiting lists.
    c. Fill new openings with walk-ins or patients from the waiting list.

3. **Follow-up**
    a. Activate a sequence of reminder calls/emails to all patients 10 days, 2 days, and 1 day prior to their appointments.
    b. Place follow-up calls to determine reasons for no-shows, and reschedule the patients.
    c. Follow up with warning letters after one no-show.
    d. Dismiss patients from the practice after three no-shows.

Reminder calls or emails prior to an appointment remain the most effective method to prevent missed appointments. Additionally, sending reminders via email and allowing patients to confirm online turns an office reminder into a patient's action item, significantly outperforming the impact of a voice message or postcard.

Note that outsourcing reminder calls to calling services and using the Internet reduce the cost of reminders. Therefore, reaching *all* patients prior to their appointments makes good business sense.

Three technologies are especially useful in implementing the no-show management strategy outlined here:

1. **End-of-day report** – End-of-day reports display new patients, visits, cash, insurance, free visits, insurance billed and collected, cash collected, missed appointments, recalls, and average patient visit. An end-of-day report allows the manager to reconcile revenues with patient visits, eliminating no-charge visits and unbillable appointments.

2. **Scheduler** – A scheduler can achieve the following:
    a. Allow patients access to an Internet-based appointment scheduler.
    b. Update the available appointment list due to cancellations.
    c. Alert about new openings for patients on the waiting list.
    d. Alert about appointments with missing authorizations.

    Most schedulers allow monthly, weekly, and daily views. The "today" view should change colors for no-show appointments, prompting the front office person to follow up immediately or at the end of the day.

3. **Search feature** – A search feature must allow you to find all no-shows within a specific time interval subject to specific patient names, attending physicians, CPT and/or ICD-9 code combinations, or other demographic conditions. Upon finding specific appointments, a "drill down" should be available to see the related appointment history or recurring appointment plan.

Chapter 44

Appointment Reminders for Revenue Protection and Patient Relationship Management

When patients miss appointments, they interrupt the flow of patient care, impede clinic productivity, and signal an eroding patient loyalty. The rate of no-shows runs at 30% for the average family practice.[114] A missed appointment amounts to missed billing revenue. Worse, if clinicians are part-time or full-time staff rather than contracted, they sit idle on the company clock, losing money with each passing minute. Finally, a missed appointment could be a symptom of a deserting patient, signaling a potential loss of long-term billing revenue.

Reminder calls for upcoming appointments and follow-up calls on recent no-shows are effective strategies for billing revenue protection because they reduce the number of no-shows and help early identification of incipient patient attrition and other patient relationship problems. Vendors of reminder call services quote no-show reduction rates

[114] Izard, "Managing the Habitual No-Show Patient."

of 50%.[115] They also mention comparable improvement of long-term patient loyalty. Other no-show reduction strategy components include charges for missed appointments, no-show statistics analysis, and overbooking.

While recognizing the benefits of reminder calls, busy practice owners often neglect or postpone reminder and follow-up calls because of other office management priorities, such as personnel issues or billing. As with any other management initiative, to get results, a reminder call strategy must be implemented systematically and consistently.

Reminder call automation delivers the benefits of billing revenue protection and patient relationship management in a disciplined and systematic fashion and at a significantly lower cost. Successful implementation of reminder call automation depends on technology and requires the following components:

1. **Flexible messaging** – A successful appointment reminder to consistently fit the culture of your practice, location, and specific appointment type. Typically, a practice uses new patient, existing patient, and recall patient messages as well as several specialty messages.

2. **Appointment scheduler integration** – A seamless method for retrieving the appointment information without involving the medical staff. Ideally, the message scheduler should be integrated within electronic medical billing software, providing transparent access to both the patient appointment scheduler and patient financial records.

3. **Call scheduling** – The ability to schedule and automati-

[115] Hashim, Franks, and Fiscella, "Effectiveness of Telephone Reminders."

cally call patients with a personalized human voice message.

4. **High-quality infrastructure** – A facility with the highest-quality fiberoptic feed, digital lines allowing unsurpassed message quality, and call progress detection accuracy. This technology helps to do the following:
    a. Avoid the pause that accompanies most automated messages. In fact, any pause after the first sound could lead a patient to hang up or lead to improper call diagnosis.
    b. Use call progress detection to determine if the phone was answered by a person or by an answering machine. This can mean the difference between leaving a complete message or only a short segment of the message on the answering machine.

Finally, when shopping for automated reminder services, focus on vendors that offer SaaS-driven service and pricing. "Software as a Service" vendors of reminder call automation solutions price their services for only the calls they make, while you avoid purchasing hardware/software and associated management and maintenance costs. In financial management terms, the SaaS proposition is equivalent to turning capital expense into operating expense, which translates into a better balance sheet and lower risk.

Glossary of Billing Terms

Account Number: A unique number that's assigned to patients when they visit a hospital or practice.

Accounts Receivable: Monies owed to a practice for delivered services.

Adjustment: A portion of the patient's bill that's adjusted by the payer due to a difference between the charged fee for service and the allowed amount, as reflected in the contract between the provider and payer.

Allowed Amount: The fee for a specific procedure or service that's in the contract/agreement between the provider and payer.

Amount Not Covered: A portion of the patient's bill that the insurance company will not pay. It may include deductibles, co-insurances, and charges for noncovered services.

Amount Payable by Plan: The amount the insurance plan pays or covers for the patient's treatment, less any deductibles, co-insurance, or charges for noncovered services.

Benefit: The services that are covered under the insurance plan.

CAP (Claims Assistance Professional): – A title used by the members of the Alliance of Claims Assistance Professionals (ACAP).

Capitated: A fixed payment system in which the physician is pre-paid monthly for enrolled members of a healthcare plan, regardless of the number of patients actually seen by the physician.

Capitated Rate: The reimbursement rate to a capitated physician.

Capitation Check: A monthly check sent to the physician from the HMO plan.

Capitation List: A list of patients enrolled in an HMO in which the physician is capitated.

CBCS (Certified Billing and Coding Specialist): A certification offered by the National Healthcare Alliance (NHA).

CHP (Certified in Healthcare Privacy): A certification offered by the American Health Information Management Association (AHIMA).

CHRS (Certified Healthcare Reimbursement Specialist): A certification offered by the National Electronic Billers Alliance (NEBA).

CMRS (Certified Medical Reimbursement Specialist): A certification offered by the American Medical Billing Association (AMBA).

CMS (Centers for Medicare and Medicaid Services): A federal agency that oversees Medicare and Medicaid.

COBRA Insurance: Health insurance coverage that patients can purchase when they're no longer employed, or when they're waiting for a new insurance plan's coverage to begin. Coverage may be purchased for up to 18 months from the termination of employment. It's generally more expensive than insurance provided through the employer, but less expensive than insurance purchased as an individual policy.

Co-insurance: The percentage of a fee not covered under an indemnity plan or original Medicare. For example, if a policy covers 80% of charges, the co-insurance/patient portion would be the remaining 20%.

Co-payment/Co-pay: A fixed fee established by the managed care plan for a specific type of visit. This amount is due from the patient. The co-pay amount is usually on the patient's insurance card, and it's different according to the type of visit. For example, an emergency room visit might be $50, an inpatient stay $100, and a physician office visit $20.

CPT (Current Procedural Terminology) Codes: Codes used to communicate level I services and procedures and HCPCS.

Date of Service (DOS): The date(s) when the patient is provided healthcare services. For an inpatient stay, the dates of service are the admission date through the discharge date. For outpatient services, the date of service is the date of the office visit.

Deductible: An amount that the insured must pay on an annual basis before the payer pays any reimbursement. This is typical to indemnity, traditional, and commercial health insurance plans.

Demographics: Personal information about the patient, including name, date of birth, gender, etc.

Denied: Refused to grant payment for a claim.

E-Codes: ICD-9 codes used to describe nonmedical factors that further describe the injury, poisoning, or other adverse reactions affecting the patient's health.

Electronic Claims Clearinghouse: An electronic claims clearinghouse accepts insurance claims and submits them to payers. Clearinghouses reduce the complexity of provider-payer connectivity. A clearinghouse is a necessary component of a seamless (built-in) system that allows a practice or billing service to submit all claims electronically and have them validated online and in almost real-time.

A clearinghouse delivers economies of scale in two important ways:

1. Saves the billing service or practice the cost of direct connection to payers
2. Expedites the revenue cycle by testing the validity of submitted claims prior to delivering them to payers

The clearinghouse receives claims, checks them for completeness and accuracy, forwards valid claims to payers, and notifies the submission source of any problems, expediting the correction process and claim resubmission.

Given N providers and M payers, a complete network of all N providers submitting claims to all M payers requires N x M connections. A clearinghouse, connected to all providers and payers, reduces the number of connections down to M + N.

Electronic Funds Transfer (EFT): A payment method in which the payer deposits funds directly into the provider's bank account.

Established Patient: A patient who has been seen by the physician in the past 36 months.

Explanation of Benefits (EOB): A notice that the provider or patient receives from the insurance company after a healthcare services claim has been processed. It explains the amounts billed, paid, denied, discounted, and not covered—and the amount owed by the patient. The EOB may also communicate information needed by the insured in order to process the claim.

False Claims Act: The FCA (31 U.S.C. § 3729–3733), also called the "Lincoln Law," is a U.S. federal law that allows non-government-affiliated people to file actions against federal contractors who are allegedly committing fraud against the government. The act of filing such actions is informally called "whistleblowing."

Fee Schedule: A list of amounts that providers are allowed to charge patients for services or procedures.

Guarantor: The person responsible paying the patient's bill.

Health Care Common Procedure Coding Systems (HCPCS): (Pronounced as in "hick-picks") A coding system used to communicate level I codes for procedures and services (CPT codes, or five-digit numeric codes), and level II codes for materials, drugs, supplies, services, and durable medical equipment (national, or five-character alphanumeric codes with one letter and four digits).

Health Insurance Portability and Accountability Act (HIPAA): A 1996 law that stipulates patients' rights about their protected health information (PHI).

Health Maintenance Organization (HMO): A pre-paid insurance plan that contracts with providers to provide healthcare services at a discounted rate. HMO services typically require prior certification, authorization, and/or referrals.

ICD-9-CM (International Classification of Diseases, 9th Revision, Clinical Modification): Codes used to communicate diagnoses, signs, and symptoms of a patient.

Indemnity (traditional or commercial health insurance) plan: A type of insurance plan that reimburses 80% of the allowed amount, and the patient pays the remaining 20%.

In-Network Insurance Participation (PAR): The physician has signed a contract with the insurance company. Generally, the payer pays less to a PAR provider, but sends the payment directly to the provider (instead of the patient).

Insured (subscriber or policyholder): The person who carries the health insurance.

Managed Care Plan: An insurance plan that includes financing, management, and delivery of healthcare services—and has a contract with hospitals, physicians, and other healthcare providers.

Medicaid: A state-administered, federal- and state-funded insurance plan for low-income families who have limited or no insurance.

Medical Biller: The person responsible for getting the provider paid by submitting the provider's charges to the appropriate party and following up on delayed or incorrect payments.

Medicare: A health insurance program for people age 65 and older, some people with disabilities under age 65, and people with end-stage renal disease (ESRD).

Medicare Part A (Hospital Insurance): Healthcare coverage for inpatient stays at participating hospitals.

Medicare Part B (Medical Insurance): Healthcare coverage for doctors' services, outpatient hospital care, and some other medical services that Part A does not cover, such as the services of physical and occupational therapists and some home healthcare.

Medigap: Medicare Supplemental Insurance, available by private insurance companies, that pays for some services not covered by Medicare A or B, including deductibles and co-insurance amounts.

Modifier: A two-character alphanumeric descriptor to signify that a procedure or service had a technical or professional component, was performed by more than one physician, had a change of scope, or had only part of a service performed.

National Provider Number (NPI): A 10-digit, intelligence-free numeric identifier. It carries no built-in information about the practice's state, payer, or specialty.

New Patient: A patient who has not been seen in the past 36 months.

Noncovered Services: Services not covered under the patient's insurance plan. These charges are the patient's responsibility to pay.

Out-of-Network Provider/Nonparticipating Provider (Non-PAR): Provider that's not part of the insurance plan's network of contracted providers. Generally, insurance plans pay more for services by an out-of-network provider, the guarantor has higher out-of-pocket costs, and the payment is made directly to the insured.

Out-of-Pocket Cost: The amount that the patient pays until the benefit coverage reaches 100%. This may include co-payment, co-insurance, or a deductible.

Outpatient: Services performed at a facility where the patient remains for less than 24 hours and is not formally admitted.

Payer: Insurance company that pays for benefits.

PHI (Protected Health Information): Personal and health information about the patient.

Point-of-Service (POS) Plan: An insurance plan that allows patients to choose doctors and hospitals without a referral from the primary care physician.

Pre-Authorization Number: Authorization given by a health plan for a member to obtain services from a healthcare provider. This is commonly required for hospital services.

Pre-Certification Number: A number obtained from the insurance company by doctors and hospitals. This number represents the insurance plan's approval for a service. This is not a guarantee of payment.

Preferred Provider Organization (PPO): An insurance plan that contracts with providers to provide healthcare services at a discounted rate. These services may require prior certification, authorization, and/or referrals.

Primary: The insurance plan that's billed first for medical services.

Primary Care Provider (PCP): A healthcare provider who is responsible for a patient's overall healthcare.

Provider: Healthcare service provider.

Rejected: Refused to accept a claim.

Referral: Approval or consent by a primary care physician for a patient to see a certain specialist or receive certain services.

Secondary (Supplemental) Plan: The insurance plan that's billed for medical services after the primary plan has (partially) paid or denied payment.

Specialist: A physician who specializes in a particular medical field.

Straight-Through Billing (STB): Electronic claims and payment processing that automatically processes the vast majority of claims and payments. STB connects the entire claims and payment processing cycle into a single integrated workflow, and it automatically flags trouble claims and payments for correction and reprocessing.

Subscriber: The person responsible for paying insurance premiums or whose employment is the basis for eligibility for a health plan membership.

Superbill (encounter form): A form that documents a patient's visit. It consists of three parts: patient demographics, insurance information, and visit data (HCPCS, ICD-9, and CPT codes; date of service; attending physician; etc.).

V Codes: ICD-9 codes assigned for preventive medical services as well as services that are required for reasons other than disease or injury.

References

Aalseth, P. T. (1999). *Codebusters: Quick Guide to Coding and Billing Compliance for Medical Practices.* Gaithersburg, MD: Aspen.

Abelson, R. (2008, February 13). New York investigates medical rate setting [Electronic version]. *The New York Times.*

American Health Information Management Association. (1999, December). *Standards of Ethical Coding.* Retrieved October 14, 2008, from http://www.ahima.org/infocenter/guidelines/standards.asp

American Health Information Management Association. (2004, July 21). *American Health Information Management Association Code of Ethics.* Retrieved October 14, 2008, from http://library.ahima.org/xpedio/groups/public/documents/ahima/bok1_024277.hcsp?dDocName=bok1_024277

American Medical Association. (2008, April). *Medicare Participation Options for Physicians.* Retrieved August 2, 2008, from http://www.ama-assn.org/ama1/pub/upload/mm/399/medicarepayment08.pdf

Ball, M. J., & Gold, J. (2006). Banking on health: Personal records and information exchange [Electronic version]. *Journal of Healthcare Information Management, 20*(2), 71–83.

Borger, C., Smith, S., Truffer, C., Keehan, S., Sisko, A., John Poisal, & Clemens, M. K. (2006, February 22). Health spending projections through 2015: Changes on the horizon. *Health Affairs Web Exclusive,* W61.

Brooks, N., & Menachemi, R. (2006). Physicians' use of email with patients: Factors influencing electronic communication and adherence to best practices. *Journal of Medical Internet Research, 8*(1), e2.

Bruderlin, F. (2003). TriCity Medical Center gives its cash flow problem a shot in the arm. *Healthcare Biller: The Communication Network for America's Health Care Billers, 12*(1).

Buppert, C. (2005). *The Primary Care Provider's Guide to Compensation and Quality: How to Get Paid and Not Get Sued.* Sudbury, MA: Jones and Bartlett.

Burgos, M., Johnson, D., & Keogh, J. (2006). *Medical Billing & Coding Demystified*. New York: McGraw-Hill.

Burrill, G. S. (2007, September). *Biotech 2007: A Global Transformation.* Presentation at meeting of the National Institute of Standards and Technology, Gaithersburg, MD. Retrieved September 8, 2008, from http://www.itl.nist.gov/Healthcare/conf/presentations/092507TUE%20NIST%20Conference%20in%20Gaithersburg.pdf

Bush, G. W. (2004, January 26). President Bush calls for medical liability reform. Speech at Baptist Health Medical Center, Little Rock, AR. Retrieved January 4, 2008, from http://www.whitehouse.gov/news/releases/2004/01/20040126-3.html

Capko, J. (2007, June). Physicians practice pearls: You earned it, now collect it [Electronic version]. *Physicians Practice.*

Capra, B., Lirov, Y., & Randolph, J. (2006, December). The "business" of healthcare provider audits—How payers are getting away with practice murder. *Today's Chiropractic*, 60–62.

Catlin, A., Cowan, C., Heffler, & S., Washington, B. (2006). National health spending in 2005. *Health Affairs, 26*(1), 142–153.

Centers for Medicare and Medicaid Services, U.S. Department of Health and Human Services. (n.d.). *National Correct Coding Initiatives Edits.* Retrieved October 14, 2008, from http://www.cms.hhs.gov/NationalCorrectCod InitEd

Centers for Medicare and Medicaid Services, U.S. Department of Health and Human Services. (n.d.). *Recovery Audit Contractor Overview.* Retrieved March 25, 2008, from http://www.cms.hhs.gov/RAC

Chan, G. (2008, January 30). PacifiCare fined record $3.5 million [Electronic version]. *The Sacramento Bee*, p. D1.

Collins, J. (2001). *Good to Great: Why Some Companies Make the Leap . . . and Others Don't.* New York: HarperCollins.

Delman, I. (2002). *The Business of Chiropractic: How to Prosper After Startup* (2nd ed.). Dandridge, TN: Business of Chiropractic Publications.

Donato, S. (2003, April). Three steps to fewer denials: Getting claims management under control [Electronic version]. *Physicians Practice.*

Dubin, C. H. (2004). A one-two punch: Drug/medical device combination products are taking healthcare in a new direction. Is the pharmaceutical industry prepared? [Electronic version]. *Drug Delivery Technology, 4*(4).

Ernst & Young. (2006, April 4). *Double-digit Growth Pushes Biotechnology Industry Revenues Over $60 Billion.* http://www.ey.com/GLOBAL/content.nsf/International/Media_-_Press_Release_-_Beyond_Borders_2006

Espicom Business Intelligence. (2006, August 24). *Research and Markets: The USA Is Home to Most of the World's Major Manufacturers, Such as Pfizer, Merck & Co and Bristol-Myers Squibb.* Retrieved September 8, 2008, from the BNET Business Network website: http://findarticles.com/p/articles/mi_m0EIN/is_2006_August_24/ai_n26967360

False Claims Act, 31 U.S.C. § 3729–3733 (1986).

Freking, K. (2008, March 1). Audits sting hospitals, physicians [Electronic version]. *USA Today.*

Fuhrmans, V. (2007, February 14). Billing battle: Fights over health claims spawn a new arms race. *The Wall Street Journal* (Eastern edition), p. A1.

Fuhrmans, V., & Francis, T. (2008, February 14). Probe targets health insurers on payments [Electronic version]. *The Wall Street Journal.*

Gerber, M. E. (1995). *The E-Myth Revisited: Why Most Small Businesses Don't Work and What to Do About It.* New York: HarperCollins.

Girion, L. (2008, June 17). AMA calls physician reimbursements flawed [Electronic version]. *The Los Angeles Times.*

Glendinning, D. (2007, December 24/31). Looming Medicare pay cut forces tough decisions on participation [Electronic version]. *American Medical News.*

Goulding, M. R., Rogers, M. E., & Smith, S. M. (2003). Public Health and Aging: Trends in Aging—United States and Worldwide [Electronic version]. *MMWR Weekly, 52*(6), 101–106.

Guglielmo, W. J. (2001, January 22). Prompt-pay laws are finally getting teeth. *Medical Economics.*

Hashim, M., Franks, P., & Fiscella, K. (2001). Effectiveness of telephone reminders in improving rate of appointments kept at an outpatient clinic: A randomized controlled trial. *Journal of the American Board of Family Practice, 14*(3), 193–196.

Healthcare Financial Management Association. (2003). *Tip Sheet: Medical Claims Denial Management.* Westchester, IL: Author.

Health Insurance Portability and Accountability Act (HIPAA), 42 U.S.C. 1320. (1996). Retrieved September 8, 2008, from http://www.hipaaprivacyworkgroups.com/Regs/Privacy%20Regs%20TOC.htm

Henry J. Kaiser Family Foundation. (2006, September 26). *Employee Health Benefits 2006 Annual Survey.* Retrieved October 14, 2008, from http://www.kff.org/insurance/7527

Henry J. Kaiser Family Foundation. (2006, September 26). *Health Insurance Premium Growth Moderates Slightly in 2006, But Still Increases Twice as Fast as Wages and Inflation.* Retrieved September 8, 2008, from http://www.kff.org/insurance/ehbs092606nr.cfm

Henry J. Kaiser Family Foundation. (2007, October). *The Uninsured: A Primer – Key Facts About Americans Without Health Insurance.* Retrieved September 8, 2008, from http://www.kff.org/uninsured/upload/7451-03.pdf

Herzlinger, R. (2007). *Who Killed Health Care? America's $2 Trillion Medical Problem—and the Consumer-Driven Cure.* New York: McGraw-Hill.

Izard, T. (2005, February). Managing the Habitual No-Show Patient [Electronic version]. *Family Practice Management.*

Japsen, B. (2008, June 17). AMA rates health insurers: Speed, accuracy in claims work graded [Electronic version]. *Chicago Tribune.*

Kinsella, K., & Velkoff, V. (2001). *An Aging World: 2001* (series P95/01-1). Washington, DC: U.S. Government Printing Office.

Kotter, J. P. (1996). *Leading Change.* Boston: Harvard Business School Publishing.

Laub, G., & Lirov, Y. (2006). The game of medical billing in today's cardiology practice. *EP Lab Digest, 6*(4), 8–9.

Lirov, Y. (1997). *Mission-Critical Systems Management.* Upper Saddle River, NJ: Prentice Hall.

Lirov, Y. (2006). 5-step lockbox selection for outsourced electronic medical billing software and service. Retrieved August 2, 2007, from http://ezinearticles.com/?5-Step-Lockbox-Selection-for-Outsourced-Electronic-Medical-Billing-Software-and-Service&id=292801

Lirov, Y. (2006). 7-step chiropractic office billing precision software for result-driven patient care plan. Retrieved August 2, 2007, from http://ezinearticles.com/?7-Step-Chiropractic-Office-Billing-Precision-Software-For-Result-Driven-Patient-Care-Plan&id=283199

Lirov, Y. (2006). 8-step plan for software and practice integration of electronic medical billing service + SaaS EMR . Retrieved August 2, 2007, from http://ezinearticles.com/?8-Step-Plan-for-Software-and-Practice-Integration-of--Electronic-Medical-Billing-Service-+-SaaS-EMR-&id=319226

Lirov, Y. (2006). Best-of-breed medical billing service + SaaS EMR-8 software and practice transition challenges. Retrieved August 2, 2007, from http://ezinearticles.com/?Best-Of-Breed-Medical-Billing-Service-+-SaaS-EMR---8-Software-and-Practice-Transition-Challenges&id=317981

Lirov, Y. (2006). Centralized workflow management for outsourced electronic medical billing service and software. Retrieved August 2, 2007, from http://ezinearticles.com/?Centralized-Workflow-Management-for-Outsourced-Electronic-Medical-Billing-Service-and-Software&id=214866

Lirov, Y. (2006). Chiropractic office billing software and patient relationship management—9 criteria for best SaaS. Retrieved August 2, 2007, from http://ezinearticles.com/?Chiropractic-Office-Billing-Software-And-Patient-Relationship-Management---9-Criteria-For-Best-SaaS&id=

309747

Lirov, Y. (2006). Computer aided patient scheduling for improved medical billing service performance. Retrieved August 2, 2007, from http://ezinearticles.com/?Computer-Aided-Patient-Scheduling-for-Improved-Medical-Billing-Service-Performance&id=236317

Lirov, Y. (2006). Electronic medical billing dashboard software—9 performance indicators for service outsourcing. Retrieved August 2, 2007, from http://ezinearticles.com/?Electronic-Medical-Billing-Dashboard-Software---9-Performance-Indicators-For-Service-Outsourcing&id=301114

Lirov, Y. (2006). Electronic medical billing OLAP software for lost revenue discovery. Retrieved August 2, 2007, from http://ezinearticles.com/?Electronic-Medical-Billing-OLAP-Software-for-Lost-Revenue-Discovery&id=248675

Lirov, Y. (2006). Electronic medical billing software and service compliance with pre-payment and post-payment audits. Retrieved August 2, 2007, from http://ezinearticles.com/?Electronic-Medical-Billing-Software-and-Service-Compliance-With-Pre-Payment-And-Post-Payment-Audits&id=227773

Lirov, Y. (2006). Electronic medical billing software and service performance metrics. Retrieved August 2, 2007, from http://ezinearticles.com/?Electronic-Medical-Billing-Software-and-Service-Performance-Metrics&id=215620

Lirov, Y. (2006). Electronic medical billing software, HIPAA compliance, and role based access control. Retrieved August 2, 2007, from http://ezinearticles.com/?Electronic-Medical-Billing-Software,-HIPAA-Compliance,-and-Role-Based-Access-Control&id=250740

Lirov, Y. (2006). Electronic Straight Through Billing service and software methodology for medical practice. Retrieved August 2, 2007, from http://ezinearticles.com/?Electronic-Straight-Through-Billing-Service-and-Software-Methodology-for-Medical-Practice&id=246227

Lirov, Y. (2006). Medical billing control and compliance with computer aided coding software. Retrieved August 2, 2007, from http://ezinearticles.com/?Electronic-Medical-Billing-Control-with-Computer-Aided-Coding-Software&id=240570

Lirov, Y. (2006). Medical billing denial management – 4 step process to improve performance. Retrieved August 2, 2007, from http://ezinearticles.com/?4-Step-Denial-Management-To-Improve-Performance-Of-Electronic-Medical-Billing-Software-And-Service&id=310321

Lirov, Y. (2006). Practice perfect—10 criteria for best chiropractic billing software and office management solution. Retrieved August 2, 2007, from http://ezinearticles.com/?Practice-Perfect---10-Criteria-For-Best-Chiropractic-Billing-Software-And-Office-Management-Solution&id=306832

Lirov, Y. (2006). Problem tracking for outsourced electronic medical billing software and service. Retrieved August 2, 2007, from http://ezinearticles.com/?Problem-Tracking-For-Outsourced-Electronic-Medical-Billing-Software-And-Service&id=247225

Lirov, Y. (2006). Relative value price-performance calculation for outsourced electronic medical billing service. Retrieved August 2, 2007, from http://ezinearticles.com/?Relative-Value-Price-Performance-Calculation-for-Outsourced-Electronic-Medical-Billing-Service&id=206604

Lirov, Y. (2006). Top 3 electronic medical billing software methods for no-show and missed appointment risk reduction. Retrieved August 2, 2007, from http://ezinearticles.com/?Top-3-Electronic-Medical-Billing-Software-Methods-For-No-Show-And-Missed-Appointment-Risk-Reduction-&id=328056

Lirov, Y. (2006). Top 4 reports for patient relationship management and outsourced chiropractic office billing service. Retrieved August 2, 2007, from http://ezinearticles.com/?Top-4-Reports-For-Patient-Relationship-Management-And-Outsourced-Chiropractic-Office-Billing-Service&id=324869

Lirov, Y. (2006). Top 5 keys to physician interface dilemma in electronic medical billing and EMR software systems. Retrieved August 2, 2007, from http://ezinearticles.com/?Top-5-Keys-To-Physician-Interface-Dilemma-In-Electronic-Medical-Billing-And-EMR-Software-Systems&id=288275

Lirov, Y. (2007). Chiropractic office in 2025—Automated billing and practice management, and intelligent equipment. Retrieved August 2, 2007, from http://ezinearticles.com/?Chiropractic-Office-Workflow-In-2025---Scheduling,-Clinical-Service,-Notes,-And-Billing-Software&id=425699

Lirov, Y. (2007). Improve patient loyalty with integrated electronic medical billing, notes, and scheduling software. Retrieved August 2, 2007, from http://ezinearticles.com/?Improve-Patient-Loyalty-with-Integrated-Electronic-Medical-Billing,-Notes,-And-Scheduling-Software&id=427289

Lirov, Y. (2007). Intelligent electronic medical billing and SOAP notes software requirements. Retrieved August 2, 2007, from http://ezinearticles.com/?Intelligent-Electronic-Medical-Billing-and-SOAP-Notes-Software-Requirements&id=444444

Lirov, Y. (2007). Medical billing revenue protection—Appointment reminders and patient relationship management. Retrieved August 2, 2007, from http://ezinearticles.com/?Appointment-Reminders-for-Medical-Billing-Revenue-Protection-and-Patient-Relationship-Management&id=459864

Lirov, Y. (2007). Outsourcing dilemma of electronic medical billing software and service. Retrieved August 2, 2007, from http://ezinearticles.com/?Outsourcing-Dilemma-Of-Electronic-Medical-Billing-Software-And-Service-&id=490193

Lirov, Y. (2007). *Practicing Profitability: Billing Network Effect for Revenue Cycle Control in Healthcare Clinics and Chiropractic Offices*. Marlboro, NJ: Affinity Billing.

Lirov, Y. (2007). Top 5 strategies to improve OTC payment performance with electronic medical billing software. Retrieved August 2, 2007, from http://ezinearticles.com/?Top-5-Strategies-to-Improve-OTC-Payment-Performance-With-Electronic-Medical-Billing-Software&id=539366

Lirov, Y. (2008). Chiropractic Billing Performance Index 2007 – Ten best-paying insurance companies. Retrieved October 14, 2008, from http://ezinearticles.com/?Chiropractic-Billing-Performance-Index-2007---Ten-Best-Paying-Insurance-Companies&id=906309

Lirov, Y. (2008). Chiropractic Billing Performance Index changes leadership in August. Retrieved October 14, 2008, from http://ezinearticles.com/?Chiropractic-Billing-Performance-Index-Changes-Leadership-in-August&id=1456938

Lirov, Y. (2008). Chiropractic office billing index gains 0.8% in December – Medicare and Blues of Illinois lead. Retrieved October 5, 2008, from http://ezinearticles.com/?Chiropractic-Office-Billing-Index-Gains-0.8%25-in-December---Medicare-and-Blues-of-Illinois-Lead&id=905702

Lohr, S. (2008, June 19). Most doctors aren't using electronic health records [Electronic version]. *The New York Times.*

Lowes, R. (2004, September). Practice pointers: How to cut A/R [Electronic version]. *Medical Economics, 81*(17), 22.

Maguire, P. (2000, December). Your practice claims denied? Take steps to get what you're owed [Electronic version]. *American College of Physicians-American Society of Internal Medicine Observer.*

Marcinko, D. E. (2004). *The Business of Medical Practice: Advanced Profit Maximization Techniques for Savvy Doctors.* New York: Springer.

McKay, N. L., & Lemak, C. H. (2006). Analyzing administrative costs in hospitals. *Health Care Management Review, 31*(4):347–354.

Medical Association of Billers. (2004). *2004 Annual Medical Billing Salary and Statistics Survey.* Retrieved June 7, 2007, from http://www.e-medbill.com/biller_survey_results.htm

Medical Group Management Association. (2007). *Increases in Primary, Specialty Physician Compensation Fail to Keep Up with Inflation: Physicians Continue Working Harder for Smaller Pay Increases.* Retrieved September 8, 2008, from http://www.mgma.com/press/default.aspx?id=14286

Medical Group Management Association. (1998). *Physician Cost Survey, 1998.* Englewood, CO: Author.

Medical Group Management Association. (2005). *Performance and Practices of Successful Medical Groups: 2005 Report Based on 2004 Data.* Retrieved September 8, 2008, from http://www5.mgma.com/ecom/Default.aspx?action=INVProductDetails&args=820&tabid=138

Medical Group Management Association. (2007). *Physician Compensation and Production Survey: 2007 Report Based on 2006 Data.* Retrieved September 8, 2008, from http://www5.mgma.com/ecom/Default.aspx?action=INVProductDetails&args=2753&tabid=138

Metcalfe, R. M. (2007, May 7). It's all in your head [Electronic version]. *Forbes, 179*(10), 52–56.

Moore, C., Wilson-Witherspoon, P., & Probst, J. (2001). Time and money: Effects of no-shows at a family practice residency clinic. *Family Medicine, 33*(7), 522–527.

Moore, P. (2007, January). The 2006 fee schedule survey: Power to the payers—Consolidation puts insurers in charge [Electronic version]. *Physicians Practice*, 23–30.

National Coalition on Health Care. (2007). *Facts on Health Care Costs.* Retrieved October 5, 2008, from http://www.nchc.org/facts/2007%20updates/cost.pdf

National Coalition on Health Care. (n.d.). *Health Insurance Costs.* Retrieved January 4, 2008, from http://www.nchc.org/facts/cost.shtml

New Jersey Department of Banking and Insurance. (2007, Fall). Aetna target of record DOBI fine for health insurance provider [Electronic version]. *Banking and Insurance Quarterly.*

NewsInferno.com. (2008, February 18). *Health Insurance Companies Defrauding Consumers Critics Charge.* Retrieved October 5, 2008, from http://www.newsinferno.com/archives/2597

Office of Inspector General (OIG). (2006). *Health Care Fraud and Abuse Control Annual Report: Fiscal 2005.* Washington, DC: Author.

Office of the Attorney General, State of New York. (2008, February 13). *Cuomo Announces Industry-wide Investigation into Health Insurers' Fraudulent Reimbursement Scheme.* Retrieved October 5, 2008, from http://www.oag.

state.ny.us/media_center/2008/feb/feb13a_08.html

Overfield, W. (2008, February 10). *The Cost of Health Care Overpayments.* Retrieved October 5, 2008, from the CNO Associates website: http://cnoassociates.com/Documents/HEALTH%20CARE%20OVERPAYMENTS%20Fact%20Sheet3.doc

Pérez-Peña, R. (2006, September 11). When choice of a doctor drives up other bills [Electronic version]. *The New York Times.*

Peter, L. J., & Hull, R. (1993). *The Peter Principle: Why Things Always Go Wrong.* Cutchogue, NY: Buccaneer Books.

Phelps, D., & Serres, C. (2006, October 18). McGuire's deal is focus of U.S. Senate inquiry [Electronic version]. *Star Tribune* (Minneapolis, MN).

Reed, M. C., & Ginsburg, P. B. (2003, March). *Behind the Times: Physician Income, 1995–99* (Data Bulletin No. 24). Retrieved September 8, 2008, from Center for Studying Health System Change website: http://www.hschange.org/CONTENT/544/

Reizer, J. L., & Reizer, S. (2002). *Up and Running—Opening a Chiropractic Office.* Otsego, MI: PageFree.

Richter, S. (2007). *Combination Products: Navigating Two FDA Quality Systems.* Agawam, MA: Microtest. Retrieved August 12, 2008, from http://www.microtestlabs.com/combinationpaper/0750506ComboWhitePaper.pdf

Riddick, F. A., Jr. (2003). Code of Medical Ethics of the American Medical Association [Electronic version]. *The Ochsner Journal, 5*(2), 6–10.

Rowell, J. C., & Green, M. A. (2005). *Understanding Health Insurance: A Guide to Billing and Reimbursement* (8th ed.). Florence, KY: Thomson Delmar Learning.

Saner, R. J., Spindel, M., & Nordeng, A. (2000). *Understanding Compliance: A Program Guide Based on the OIG 2000 Guidance.* Englewood, CO: Medical Group Management Association.

Skelton, H. C. (2007, August 28). *Aetna Ordered by NJDOBI to Cease Unfair Limitation of Medicare Payments.* Retrieved October 5, 2008, from http://www.doctorslawyer.com/2007/08/28/aetna-ordered-by-njdobi-to-cease-unfair-limitation-of-medicare-payments

Snyder, L., & Leffler, D. (Eds.). (2005). *Ethics Manual* (5th ed.). Philadelphia: American College of Physicians.

Stechschulte, P. (2003). A glance into the future [Electronic version]. *Today's Chiropractic, 32*(3), 38–45.

UnitedHealth Group. (2006, October 19). UnitedHealth Group reports record third quarter net earnings of $0.79 per share. *Business Wire.* Retrieved October 5, 2008, from the AllBusiness website: http://www.allbusiness.com/services/business-services/3927347-1.html

United Nations. (2002, April). *Report of the Second World Assembly on Aging.* Madrid, Spain: Author.

U.S. Census Bureau. (2008, May 16). *U.S. Population Projections.* Retrieved October 5, 2008, from http://www.census.gov/population/www/projections/natdet-D1A.html

U.S. Department of Justice, Civil Division. (2005). *Fraud Statistics—October 1, 1986–September 30, 2004.* Washington, DC: Author.

U.S. Department of Justice. (n.d.). *False Claims Act Cases: Government Intervention in Qui Tam (Whistleblower) Suits.* Retrieved March 25, 2008, from http://www.usdoj.gov/usao/pae/Documents/fcaprocess2.pdf

U.S. Department of Justice. (2006, November 21). *Justice Department recovers record $3.1 billion in fraud and false claims in fiscal year 2006.* Retrieved October 5, 2008, from http://www.usdoj.gov/opa/pr/2006/November/06_civ_783.html

U.S. Department of Justice, U.S. Attorney's Office, District of Connecticut. (2006, December 21). *Waterbury Doctor Pays $160,000 to Settle Civil Allegations Under the False Claims Act.* Retrieved March 25, 2008, from http://www.usdoj.gov/usao/ct/Press2006/20061221-2.html

U.S. Department of Justice, U.S. Attorney's Office, District of Maryland. (2005, November 22). *Complaint Filed Against Towson Doctor for False Claims.* Retrieved March 25, 2008, from http://www.usdoj.gov/usao/md/Public-Affairs/press_releases/press05/Complaint%20Filed%20Against%20Towson%20Doctor%20for%20False%20Claims.html

U.S. Department of Justice, U.S. Attorney's Office, Northern District of Alabama. (2007, May 22). *Boaz Physician Pleads Guilty to Health Care Fraud* Retrieved March 25, 2008, from http://www.usdoj.gov/usao/aln/Docs/May%202007/may22,2007%20BOAZ%20PHYSICIAN%20PLEADS%20GUILTY.htm

U.S. Department of Justice, U.S. Attorney's Office, South District of Florida. (2007, August 20). *Former U.S. Bureau of Prisons Staff Physician, Physician's Assistant and Three Others Charged in Medicare Fraud Scheme.* Retrieved March 25, 2008, from http://www.usdoj.gov/usao/fls/PressReleases/070820-03.html

U.S. Department of Justice, U.S. Attorney's Office, South District of Texas. (2007, September 4). *U.S. Settles False Claims Act Suit.* Retrieved March 25, 2008, from http://www.usdoj.gov/usao/txs/releases/September%202007/070904-marquez_print.htm

U.S. Food and Drug Administration. (n.d.). *FY 2007 Performance Report to Congress for the Office of Combination Products as Required by the Medical Device User Fee and Modernization Act of 2002.* Retrieved September 8, 2008, from http://www.fda.gov/oc/combination/report2007.html

U.S. Government Accountability Office (GAO). *Medicare Spending: Testimony Before the Subcommittee on Health, Committee on Energy and Commerce, House of Representatives*, 110th Cong. (March 6, 2007).

Von Bergen, J. M. (2008, June 16). AMA issues report card on health insurers [Electronic version]. *Philadelphia Inquirer.*

Walker, D., Larch, S., & Woodcock, E. (2004). *The Physician Billing Process: Avoiding Potholes on the Road to Getting Paid.* Englewood, CO: Medical Group Management Association.

Wang, S. (2003). A cost-benefit analysis of electronic medical records in primary care. *The American Journal of Medicine, 114*(5), 397–403.

Waymack, P. M. (2005, January 1). Harnessing the power of e-commerce to reduce denials. *Healthcare Financial Management.* Retrieved October 14, 2008, from the AllBusiness website: http://www.allbusiness.com/personal-finance/health-care/306280-1.html

Weinberg, N. (2005, March 14). Envy engines [Electronic version]. *Forbes,*

176(5).

Wikinvest. (n.d.). *Aetna (AET)*. Retrieved September 24, 2008, from http://www.wikinvest.com/stock/Aetna_(AET)

Wikipedia. (2008). *Network Effect.* Retrieved August 1, 2008, from http://en.wikipedia.org/wiki/Network_effect

x-rates.com (n.d.). *2007 – American Dollars to 1 INR*. Retrieved October 5, 2008, from http://www.x-rates.com/d/USD/INR/hist2007.html

Index

About the Author

Yuval Lirov, PhD, is the author of *Practicing Profitability: Billing Network Effect for Revenue Cycle Control in Healthcare Clinics and Chiropractic Offices* (Affinity Billing, 2007) and *Mission-Critical Systems Management* (Prentice Hall, 1997). He is the inventor of patents in artificial intelligence and computer security, and he's CEO of Vericle, a distributed practice management and billing network technologies company.

Prior to co-founding Vericle, Lirov managed technology at Lehman Brothers, Salomon Smith Barney, and Bell Laboratories. He earned his doctorate in systems science and mathematics under the guidance of Professor E. Y. Rodin at Washington University in St. Louis.

www.ingramcontent.com/pod-product-compliance
Lightning Source LLC
LaVergne TN
LVHW102008210926
848483LV00010B/161
9780979610134